Never Alone in the Back:
A Paramedic's Reflections on Faith, Prayer and the Journey with God

By

Gerald Morton,
NREMT-P

Never Alone in the Back:
A Paramedic's Reflections on Faith, Prayer and the Journey with God

By

Gerald Morton,
NREMT-P

PUBLISHED IN THE UNITED STATES

By

Aaron Book Publishing
Bristol, Tennessee
April 2011
Sales Orders (423) 212-1208
First Edition, First Printing

Cover Design: Kellie Warren-Underwood

Disclaimer

This document is an original work of the author. It may include reference to information commonly known or freely available to the general public. Any resemblance to other published information is purely coincidental. The author has in no way attempted to use material not of his own origination. Aaron Book Publishing disclaims any association with or responsibility for the ideas, opinions or facts as expressed by the author of this book.

Printed in the United States of America
Cataloging-in-Publication
ISBN: 978-1-58275-312-6
Copyright Gerald William Morton 2011

ALL RIGHTS RESERVED

Acknowledgements

I have always called it, with no particular originality, the Job question: "Why?" In fact, I have been amazed during my now over 35 years of reading and teaching great literature, how often a play, story, or poem could be interpreted as presenting a variation on the Job question. From the poetic feet of Milton and Anne Bradstreet, to the finely crafted prose of James Joyce, we see that question take shape: "Why does a loving God allow us to suffer such horrible pain and loss?" When my children witnessed their mother's dying at a young age, I saw them wrestle with this question.

Since becoming a paramedic, I have seen the Job question take shape not on the pages of a text or in the hearts of my children, but in the lives of strangers. No matter the situation, we can identify with Job when he asked, knowing that he had why should he lose his wealth, his family, and his health.

I have grown to realize that the Job question is not the essential question for giving meaningful context for viewing our lives and understanding our relationship with God. Rather, we should ask, "How can we, with all our flaws, deserve God's love, a love so profound that he sacrificed his only son to demonstrate to us how precious we are?" This is not the Job question, but it *is* the essential question. In the pages that follow, I ask that you join me in seeing the miracle of God's love. It is a miracle so profound and fundamental that it allowed me to finally realize that it is not in the suffering Job, but rather that of Christ, that we can finally understand God's love. While focusing on the Job question gave me a wonderful vehicle for teaching literature, turning my focus to the Jesus answer gave me the more important vehicle for understanding my life. Placing my focus on Job for more than thirty-five years caused me to turn inward where I dwelled on my needs; finally placing my focus on Jesus began to help me shift my vision outwardly, beyond myself, to others, to their needs, and more importantly to the basic goodness of God's children.

I intended this book to be a celebration of others, and if I have written successfully, it will be just that. Many, who received little or no acknowledgment within the text, however, deserve mention, and I would be remiss to not thank them here.

To Steve, the finest friend a person could have, I say thank you. Your gift of joy is infectious. Your kindness, the ability you have to do for others, makes you unique. I cannot imagine having faced the dark days of my life without your friendship.

I want to thank Rosemary, Alan, and Rebecca. I am sorry that I missed your vigils at the hospital, but please know how much your being there meant to me when I finally came out of the coma and to my family whom you touched with your love.

In the EMS world I have found a special family. They, as well as the firefighters and police who respond when we dial 911, are often called "our heroes." They deserve these words. I wish particularly to thank Jay Gouge, Mark Smith, Daryl Meers, Dallis Johnson, and Jack Reedy, who have given me so much help as I have attempted to become an able paramedic.

For Jason, Larry, and the Aldersgate United Methodist Church family--how blessed I was to find you and what an amazing testimony you are to the passage "whenever two or more are gathered in his name, there is love." God walks with you every day, and your lives are witness to Him.

Once again, I find myself thanking Susan Malone, who has taught me so much about the craft of writing. She is an amazing mentor.

Finally, for my wife JeDonne, I can simply say thank you for the faith you have had in this project. Without you, it would have remained an idea, but never become a finished text. You have referred to it as "God's book." It is also yours.

Gerald Morton, NREMT-P
February 2011

For Sami

Whosoever humbles himself like this child, he is greatest in the kingdom of heaven. Matthew 18:4

You raise me up, so I can stand on mountains;
You raise me up, to walk on stormy seas;
I am strong, when I am on your shoulders;
You raise me up... To more than I can be.

--Josh Groban, "You Raise Me Up"

Prologue

Waking up in a motel room on Christmas morning is probably no one's idea of how to begin a day of celebrating the birth of our Savior and spending time with our families. My wife and I, however, had done just that after two days of driving from our cabin in the North Carolina Mountains to Michigan, where we would be visiting her family.

We had made the trip slowly. I was recovering from surgery and needed frequent stops to walk around and lessen the danger of a blood clot forming. Freezing, snowy weather demanded that we take even more precautions, including spending one night on the road before arriving in Grand Rapids and checking into the Hampton Inn on Christmas Eve. The snow that blanketed the mountains of West Virginia and the fields of Ohio and Michigan beautifully reflected the season, but would have been much easier to enjoy if we were not negotiating icy roads and high winds. Perhaps the most difficult part of this holiday journey, however, was that it was taking me away from my children. My younger daughter had tried to sneak in a quick trip from Atlanta a few days earlier, but an early December snow left the mountain roads in North Carolina impassable, blocking even that pre-holiday visit.

When my cell phone rang Christmas morning, and I saw on the screen an unfamiliar phone number from Virginia, I wasn't eager to answer. In fact, I initially tolerated the annoying ring tone until I had missed the call.

The caller, however, was persistent. The phone rang again. A second time, I hesitated to take the call. Anyone in Virginia I might want to want to talk with, especially on Christmas morning, would have been programmed into the phone. A name would have appeared, not a familiar area code with an unfamiliar number. But no name flashed on the screen. I answered anyway.

"Mr. Morton, this is Junior Musick."

I had spoken to Junior Musick once, briefly, and without, at the time, even knowing his name. On this Christmas morning a few months later, I knew his name; I knew it well. I could not have been more surprised to be receiving a call from him, especially on Christmas morning.

"Mr. Morton, I just wanted to call and tell you Sami has finished opening her presents. She opened mine and my wife's too. We wanted to say thank you. Thank you for our daughter."

I could not have imagined receiving such a Christmas gift. Tears crawled down my cheeks as Junior Musick and I visited a bit longer, discussing the night his daughter Samantha had been injured in a serious car crash as well as her long path to recovery. He told me that she had made considerable progress with her cognitive skills, but was still struggling with her motor functions. Despite her limitations, he told me, she had, like any other five-year-old, torn through the wrapping paper that stood between her and her presents, before turning her attention to her parents' gifts. Junior Musick explained how on Christmas day he and his family felt blessed that they had her with them at all. He then said that they believed I was the reason she had survived the transport to the hospital. He was giving me more credit than I deserved, but I accepted his thanks. His words left me with a full and grateful heart.

My wife, JeDonne, quickly picked up from my end of the conversation and the tears in my eyes what had just happened, and before I had finished talking with Mr. Musick was holding me in her arms. If ever I had realized that Christmas day is about miracles, I knew it that morning in Grand Rapids, Michigan, for surely God had visited that room at the Hampton Inn. His presence was palpable and overwhelming. He blessed me and my wife with the true gift of the season--a reminder of His love and His mercy. God was there in our room, just as he had been at the scene of the car wreck the night Sami Musick became a part of my life.

Chapter One

Sami Musick entered my life on a warm, March evening in 2009. The first time I saw her, first responders had extricated her from the car in which she had been a passenger and were securing her to a pediatric immobilization board. My partner Richard and I had been dispatched to a motor-vehicle collision, an MVC, but had received no information about our potential patients. As Richard positioned our truck, I jumped from the ambulance and ran to Sami, a tiny, five-year-old with silky blonde hair.

Her left pupil was blown and her right pupil dilated and fixed. It was a face to freeze the blood of the most experienced paramedic. And yet, as I would learn in the weeks that followed, it was also the face of God.

Sami had suffered multiple skull fractures. The slightest touch produced crepitus, the harsh grating sound of bone rubbing against bone. It is a sound that will awaken even a hardened paramedic at night. And yet, in that sound, I would learn, was the voice of God.

Five months later, after extensive and at times exhausting rehabilitation therapy, when Sami enrolled in the first grade, I learned the true nature of the mercy of God. And in those long months between the car wreck that almost killed their child and Christmas morning, a mother and father never lost their faith that they and their child were precious to God. In their faith we surely can see the nature of God's love for us and the one great truth about a Christian's relationship with that loving God--it is a relationship that must begin and end with faith. The words of Isaiah speak to the kind of faith the Musick family found, even in the nightmare of their daughter's injuries: "Behold, God is my salvation; I will trust, and will not be afraid; for the Lord God is my strength and my song, and he has become my salvation" (Isaiah 12:2).

On that Christmas morning, Junior Musick and his wife chose to share with me their faith and thank me for something that I knew God, not I, had done when He chose to make manifest in Sami Musick the true nature of His love, much as He had done on the first Christmas morning when He gave the gift of His son to a world desperate to believe—to believe that through faith the seeming chasm between man and God could be crossed. That through faith, the love of God and His constant presence in our lives can become obvious to us. That through faith we can navigate the most difficult moments in our lives, even those when we are desperate to understand how God could love us and still allow us to suffer. That through faith, through the faith that Jesus inspired us to hold, we can learn to see that our suffering, as much as our joy, can bring us closer to God.

*****

Every paramedic I know will admit to having the same reaction to a dispatch that indicates the patient is a child, especially if the injury is a burn, the result of a car wreck, or the rare cardiac or respiratory arrest. The more experienced the medics, the more likely they are to respond to those dispatches calmly, with confidence. But gifted medics are like skilled athletes. When the game is on the line, the exceptional athlete wants to have the bat in his hands, to take the shot, to be in position to make the play. Medics are the same. The really special ones want the calls that matter. Jokingly, in the EMS world, they are called "paragods." From what I have seen, "paragods" are more often than not the paramedics you want getting off the truck when your life, or the life of someone you love, is at risk. You may not like them. You may find their no-nonsense style as they deal with the emergency abrasive. But they are the ones who will save your life or the life of your loved one, the life of your child, and then later show the side of their personality that led them to become medics--the caring side. The side that leads them to work in a profession with significant challenges and often difficult-to-find rewards.

The night Richard and I were dispatched to the car wreck in which Sami was injured, I was not yet a paramedic and had less than two year's experience as an EMT-Intermediate. I had almost completed my last semester before testing for my medic certification and had been cleared to perform most advanced life-support protocols. I had, however, logged relatively little field time to hone my skills and harden my emotions. Dispatch had not given us any indication about the number of patients we would have or the severity of their injuries—all we had to work with to prepare in route was a location where the county responders needed ALS, advanced life support, assistance. Although I had no time mentally or emotionally to prepare myself to treat a child, much less one so seriously injured, as I think back my ignorance was a blessing. I may not have had time to prepare, but neither was there time to experience any kind of reticence about what Richard and I would be facing.

That blessing of ignorance was short-lived, however, for as we arrived on scene, Dispatch told us that MedFlight had a chopper in the air. Whenever the county crew requested a "bird," whatever was waiting was serious. When I saw Sami being immobilized by the county crew on scene, I realized how serious. When I saw her face illuminated by the headlights from cars gathered at the intersection at which the accident occurred, I experienced that long moment when something has to take over to compensate for the natural reactions of fear and uncertainty, both of which want to control such situations. And will if we let them. Fortunately, the training took over and shaped my responses, just as it is intended.

The first challenge for those of us who work in EMS in any emergency situation is not to let that situation take control of us and dictate our actions, or to let the adrenaline surge, which so often occurs, overwhelm our thought processes. In fact, the best first reaction is often not to rush to action, but rather to pause a moment, take a breath, and bring calm to a situation that is anything but calm, which is often a chaotic frenzy. I found developing the ability to "capture" that calm one of the particularly difficult challenges I had faced as a new EMS provider. I find, still, that on some calls keeping calm remains my primary focus.

Although much of what happened that night was new to my experience in EMS and challenged me in ways that I had not yet been challenged, one part of it had an eerie familiarity . . .

* * * * *

Four years earlier, I was living in Alabama, bringing my teaching career to an end and taking the classes to qualify to test for my EMT-Basic certification. The end-of-semester course requirements included spending forty hours on an ambulance, mainly observing. Sherry Meacham, my preceptor, did not believe in hauling observers around in the back of her truck and expected me to help on calls in whatever way she thought appropriate. That expectation included working with her when dispatched on a warm spring night to a drive-by shooting with multiple victims. Hers was the first ambulance to arrive. The scene was a morbid carnival as the decorations and music of a Saturday-night street party merged with the gruesome reality of a crime scene.

Bodies lay in the street or on the sidewalk. Police cars with flashing lights had isolated the victims as best they could, and fire units were on scene, illuminating the streets with their floodlights. Officers, significantly outnumbered by a large and electrified crowd, tried to keep the bystanders from interfering with the responding units and personnel. A muscled, black firefighter (who looked more like a linebacker than a medic) waved to us as we arrived. He had begun resuscitation efforts on a young black woman who had a small entrance wound just above her left eye. I followed Sherry and took over chest compressions, thus freeing the fire medic to assist her with the tasks that I was not able to perform. With help from other firefighters, we loaded our patient in the ambulance. While the fire medic, whose name I never learned, placed her on high flow O_2 and the cardiac monitor, Sherry started the first of two large gauge IVs and began a fluid bolus. She efficiently intubated our patient. The monitor showed the patient to be in asystole—she was flat lined, a rhythm which does not respond to electricity—so Sherry opened the drug box and began to administer epinephrine and atropine. Outside the open back doors, the young woman's parents and three children were screaming for us to help her. A firefighter stepped in, closed up the truck, and waved our driver to get off the scene.

I had spent the last thirty-five years in the front of a classroom teaching. Crime scenes and the back of the ambulance were not my element. I was just a student. While Sherry and the fire medic worked with calm efficiency, my heart raced and sweat poured down my face. The contrast startled me. But I learned that night the most important lesson I could learn as a student while on scene at that call. I was aware of what was happening around me--of the jostling in the crowd, the flashing of emergency unit lights, the screaming of panicked loved ones. But suddenly the noises vanished, the images that were trying to flash in my head faded to the background, and I was able to keep my focus on doing exactly what Sherry told me to do.

Our patient was dead, and nothing Sherry and the fire medic were able to do was going to change that. They "worked" her throughout the transport to the hospital. Only there, in the emergency room, did I finally see the extent of her injury. A large portion of the back of her head was missing. The ER doctor determined that she had been dead so long that even harvesting her organs would be a waste of time.

That night held no miracles, not for the daughter of frantic parents and the mother of hysterical children who had seen her shot dead as they were enjoying the arrival of spring at a neighborhood gathering.

However, on that night I learned that God had given me the ability not to let the fear and uncertainty, which are part of EMS, stand between me and doing the job that I was training to do. I did get sick in the ER and had to slip away from the crowd which rapidly gathered before losing the contents of my stomach. However, I did not abandon my journey to becoming an EMT-Basic. My goal at this point was to gain the certification level necessary to be a volunteer in the isolated North Carolina community to which I was moving. I could not have imagined that night in Alabama that my plans would change, that I would one day be the ALS provider, and that I had just finished rehearsing for many nights to come. Especially the night that Sami Musick became my patient.

* * * * *

EMS students spend a lot of time studying preset protocols and procedures to follow in a variety of situations. Almost from day one, we are admonished that personal safety trumps all other considerations. We are drilled on the ABCs of EMS: Airway, Breathing, Circulation. We memorize the diagnostic mnemonics SAMPLE (Signs & Symptoms, Allergies, Medications, Pertinent Past History, Last Oral Intake, Events Leading to Present Emergency), DCAP-BTLS (Deformity, Contusions, Abrasions, Punctures, Burns, Tenderness, Lacerations, Swelling), and OPQRST pain assessment (Onset, Provocation, Quality, Radiation, Severity, Time).

We learn additional rapid trauma and medical assessment procedures. We study extensively the Advanced Cardiac Life Support algorithms of the American Heart Association. We anticipate using these procedures often and understand their value. They allow us to respond to the most difficult calls without having to "think" through a treatment plan cold.

We also study multiple casualty incident (MCI) protocols as prescribed by NIMS (National Incident Management System). Most of us tend to consider that material necessary to learn in order to pass our certification tests, but not really something which we will ever use. After I took a quick look at Sami, I found myself using the MCI protocols. The automatic responses that the hours of classroom study cultivate kicked in. Although we had not formally established ourselves as Incident Command, Richard and I began triage. We determined that we had seven patients, six from the car from which Sami had been extricated and the driver of the other vehicle. They were all walking and talking, with what seemed, at most, minor injuries. Based on basic triage protocols, Sami did not have the respiratory effort or mental status to be considered a viable patient. She was a candidate to be black tagged using the standard START (Simple Triage and Rapid Treatment) triage system taught EMS providers. She might not survive until we reached the hospital. She had no chance to survive if we did not leave immediately. I did not have to ask Richard what he thought. We were going to get her to the emergency room as quickly as possible. It never even went through my mind to do anything else.

The decisions that I had to make in order to focus on her followed rapidly. Even though a city park with open fields about a mile away would have provided a perfect location, we did not have adequate personnel to send any first responders from the scene to set up a night landing zone for the MedFlight unit. I called Dispatch and indicated we would not need a chopper.

I asked for additional ambulances. Their best response times would be approximately fifteen minutes. I did a quick final check with the other patients to verify that they would be able to wait for the units in route for further assessment and treatment. And then I met Earl Musick.

"I'm taking your daughter. We'll be at Regional Medical Center."

I don't remember his words. He may have said nothing at all. I do remember his wide eyes, slightly opened mouth, and slack jaw. I remember his unspoken plea. His desperation. I remember the nod of his head that made clear his readiness to place Sami in my care.

Richard and I loaded Sami, left the county firefighters in charge of the scene until additional medical units arrived, and began a priority transport to the hospital. I had time to get a blood pressure and an EKG on Sami before she began to vomit, a predictable response to her head injury. I tilted the pediatric board so that Sami was lying on her right side and spent the entire transport to the hospital suctioning her airway. No fancy advanced life-support stuff. I wasn't even able to assist her breathing with a bag/valve mask. I was able to cut off the end of a nasal cannula connected to an oxygen tree and use the tube to provide blow by oxygen for Sami while I was handling the suction catheter with my other hand. I managed a quick radio report to let the ER know what to expect. I was able to maintain her airway. I was able to pray. If I had learned one thing in the less than two years I had been working as an ALS provider, it was that I am never alone in the back of an ambulance. I had learned the lesson of Proverbs 3:5-6. "Trust in the Lord with all your heart, and do not rely on your own insight. In all ways acknowledge Him, and He will make straight your paths."

Over time as an EMS provider, I have learned to trust my abilities. I have, however, also learned that the ultimate care in all situations is provided by the guiding hand of God for whom I must be an instrument. I had learned this lesson very quickly after joining the Lifesaving Crew.

* * * * *

As a member of the Lifesaving Crew for less than a month, I responded to my first major dispatch "without a net." I had run some serious calls, but always with the help of a unit from the Fire Department, with one of the fire medics on duty available to assist on scene or during transport when a patient's condition warranted the attention of two ALS providers. On this call, however, my partners and I were responding to assist county first responders. As with the night Richard and I responded to the car wreck in which Sami had been injured, we would have the assistance of first responders, but no advanced life support providers.

The dispatch was for a patient who had taken advantage of our first cool dry day in a week to cut firewood. He had been struck in the head by a falling tree. We had a fifteen to twenty minute response time, which left the opportunity to think about the challenge. About the fact that the net was gone. About how this time my job was to be the only ALS medical responder. My "orientation" was over. Moving quickly along a winding country road only enhanced the unsettled feeling that was developing in my stomach.

On the way to the scene, I learned from Dispatch that MedFlight had a chopper in route. The county crew had obviously concluded that the patient was emergent and needed a more rapid transport to the hospital than we could provide. Our job would be to treat and package the patient before air transport.

We arrived to find several first-responder units on scene and were waved to a far corner of a steeply inclined meadow. After driving as far as we could, we discovered that the patient was about 500 yards in the distance, up a steep slope, through a dense forest. The ground, wet from recent rain, oozed water like a wet sponge under our boots. Under different circumstances, I would have enjoyed the cool autumn air and the reds and yellows that had begun to paint the leaves, a signal of that time of year when the mountains of Appalachia display their brilliance with particular grandeur.

I had two partners that day. While Harold moved the ambulance to a better load position, Leslie and I began the climb, with our cot and gear in tow. The slope was too steep and the terrain became too rough to continue with the cot. We were, however, able to see the first responders working with the patient. They had the primary immobilization equipment we needed. We labored on up the hill, blowing hard as we climbed.

Our patient, a young, tall, and stoutly built man, was still face down. The first responders had taken the initial steps to immobilize his c-spine, but nothing more. I applied a c-collar to stabilize his thick neck. We straightened his left arm and first rolled him to his side and brushed the ground debris from his nose and mouth. I cut away the back of his shirt to make sure that we would not be hiding an injury that needed attention when we lowered him to the long board. Two of the first responders positioned the board snuggly against his side and we lowered him to a supine position. He was so large that the board disappeared under his bulk.

As always, the first thing a critical patient's face reveals is the need to treat immediately and to transport quickly. He was not responding to any stimulus, verbal or physical. Even when I dug a knuckle into his sternum and pressed hard, he did not react. His pupils were pinpoint. His pulse was erratic. His breathing was shallow and irregular.

We had no straps to secure him to the long board, but I had three-inch tape in my pocket. My former teacher, Toby, would have been proud, as I began to secure my patient to the long board, I could see the flush in Toby's round cheeks and hear his high-pitched voice: "Always carry three-inch tape, I'm telling you! You're gonna be glad you did one day!" A few quick rounds of tape secured our patient. We had enough first responders to carry him out. In that small, country community, they all knew him and were eager to do whatever needed to be done, including keeping a firm grasp on the long board for the slow climb down the steep ridge with a patient who would have weighed in at close to 300 pounds..

I left Leslie to guide the movement of the patient down the slope and returned to our cot and gear to prepare to treat, and to get an update about MedFlight's estimated time of arrival (ETA). The chopper was putting down at a church parking lot about a mile away, with an ETA of ten minutes. Because of the distance from the hospital to their community, county first responders are experienced with and skilled at setting up landing zones. They had taken care of the landing-zone arrangements while I had been with the patient.

By the time my patient was secured to the cot for the final descent, I was able to provide him with high-flow oxygen. I managed to reassess as we crawled down the slope, guiding the wheels of the cot over limbs and across rain-softened ground,. His symptoms suggested a skull fracture and very likely an intracranial bleed. The only significant treatment we might offer, after immobilization, was to place our patient on high-flow oxygen, transport him quickly, and prepare him for the flight in the event that his condition deteriorated.

Finally in the truck, I found myself with Kevin, a former classmate and one of the local first responders whose arrival on scene was a gift. He was not just a familiar face; he was a man whose EMT-Basic skills I trusted.

We managed to confirm a sinus heart rhythm at a slowing rate, increased blood pressure, rapid but irregular respirations, and continued unresponsiveness. He exhibited what is called Cushing's triad, an almost certain sign of intracranial pressure from a bleed within the cranial vault. He needed not just an emergency room; he needed immediate transport to a level 1 trauma center where a neurosurgical team would be not just on call but available in the hospital. Such a hospital was in Johnson City, Tennessee, an hour's drive for our ambulance, even running hot, but just a few minutes away by air. The first responders' decision to ask for a MedFlight unit had been exactly right and may well have saved our patient's life.

Trauma patients routinely receive fluid support, but with one whose blood pressure was up and who was likely bleeding into the brain, I knew not to give a fluid bolus. I also knew, however, that should his condition change, should he go into cardiac arrest in route and need IV drugs, it would be easier for me to gain IV access than it would be for a flight medic in cramped quarters once leaving the scene. I needed to begin a saline drip at KVO (Keep Vein Open) before turning him over to the flight crew.

After cutting away the sleeves of my patient's bright flannel shirt, I looked for a vein. Nothing. Just a large, muscled arm. I blindly inserted an 18 gauge needle where a vein "should" be and watched in amazement as the reservoir on the needle filled with blood. In moments, I had threaded the catheter into the vein and attached a saline lock, connected a bag of normal saline, and secured the catheter--just in time to unload the patient, give a quick report to the flight medic, help him and his crew position the patient on the chopper, and watch as they lifted off.

As they did, it hit me: I had directed my first real ALS response without another ALS provider, managed to blindly find a vein for IV access, and seen the patient transferred to the care of a flight crew. I had been surrounded by able EMTs, including Leslie, who was so spent when the chopper lifted off that she grew sick and had to slip off behind one of the trucks for privacy.

As the MedFlight "bird" slowly lifted from the parking lot, its weight load challenged by the size of the patient and its three-person crew, and disappeared behind the screen of reds and yellows of turning leaves atop a low-lying ridge, I reflected on the most obvious fact about the entire call. Kevin and I had never been alone in the back of the truck. God's hand had been involved with everything that had happened. Jeremiah 17: 7-8 reads, "Blessed is the man who trusts in the Lord, whose trust is the Lord. He is like a tree planted by water, that sends out its roots by the stream, and does not fear when heat comes." Working in EMS has shown me that no amount of study, preparation, or experience provides enough knowledge to explain everything that can happen in an emergent situation. What EMS requires is that we accept the value of study, perform to the best of our abilities, and trust that by doing so we have done our jobs, with faith that God will not abandon us or our patients.

God's hand had been involved as Leslie, Kevin, the first

responders, and I had treated our patient, as it always is in our lives. All we need do is learn to see His involvement and feel blessed by His presence. That is much easier said than done. A great deal of writing published by Christians, from the Book of Job to Harold Kushner's *When Bad Things Happen to Good People*, with the work of such writers as C. S. Lewis in between, has grappled with the challenge of seeing God at work during the dark moments of our lives. To see God's presence in what happened to Sami Musick. To see Him at work in our own lives when we feel most alone. To be open to God's love when we ask the Job question—Why? I have, for as long as I can remember, found the Book of Job to be a fascinating study of the nature of man's relationship with God. When what I call the Job question—why must I suffer?-- became for me much more than a topic for intellectual examination and the question that defined my own life, I became a very different person in one important way. I became a person for whom living by faith became not a concept to think about, but instead, a goal to which I aspired.

Chapter Two

I probably shouldn't have been mowing the yard in the middle of a hot July day in 2001. I had been out of the rehabilitation hospital only three weeks. But the yard of my garden home was small, and I planned to mow the back one day and the front the next. To do either would take at most ten minutes. And I needed to begin feeling productive again after weeks of doing little for myself and nothing for anyone else. Still, I was quickly winded. My desire to be active was greater than my physical strength. I was not displeased when my pastor pulled into the driveway and gave me a reason to stop. Of course, I could have stopped just because it made sense to do so. As anyone who knows me will tell you, however, it is not my personality to give up on a job once started until it is complete.

I really did not know Pastor Mike Siegel. He had visited me in the hospital on one occasion. However, he had become the pastor at my church. The two pastors who preceded him had moved to their new assignments while I was in a coma, caused by complications following my heart attack. I missed Larry, and especially Jason, the associate pastor who had been so welcoming when I had begun to attend services at Aldersgate United Methodist Church only a few months earlier. But Mike certainly seemed a good man who took his pastoral-care duties seriously. And when he asked if I would speak at church about how my experience had changed my faith, I agreed without a second thought. I should have considered what I was agreeing to.

Although Mike had said "changed" my faith, maybe "affected" my faith would have been more appropriate. Having a heart attack at age forty-seven and waking up weeks later to learn that at one point my chances of surviving had been assessed at less than five percent had not changed my fundamental beliefs, but the whole experience had affected my faith. It made me even more sure than I had been before that God works in ways beyond my understanding. When I learned that a basketball player at the university where I was teaching at the time had died of a heart attack while shooting hoops in the school's gym the same week of my own crisis, I was even more convinced that I had no answers to the most basic questions that arise when we try to live a life of faith. Particularly when we are trying to live a life of faith that we have only just begun to embrace. The question haunted me: Why should a young and vigorous athlete have died, while I had survived? What could God possibly have seen in me that made it so important that I "beat the odds," extraordinary odds at that.

I have a fine education, a Ph.D. in English, with now more than thirty years of experience as a teacher and researcher. In 2000, my university had awarded me the title of Distinguished Research Professor. But on issues of religion and faith, I held no particular expertise. With no idea of what to say, I nevertheless told Mike I would be happy to speak to the congregation of my church. But I better come up with something better to say than the muddled gibberish I was thinking and had been thinking from the moment I had awakened a few weeks earlier in the hospital, realized what had happened, and begun trying to make peace with the resulting spiritual trauma.

My dilemma was heightened by my reaction to the inherent conflict between the two things that had been repeated, over and over, as the wonderful people from my community, especially my church, had visited with me during my recovery. They either said that I had been lifted up by prayer, or that it was not God's plan for me to die at this point, that I still had something to do in this life. Both messages seem consistent with Christian faith. But they contradict each other. If it was God's plan that I survive, then why should the prayers said for me have mattered? If the prayers mattered to God, then clearly He had not made a decision on my fate in advance.

And then there is the arrogance that accompanies any thoughts that our individual fates are so significant in the scheme of things that God treats them with His particular interest. To me, this conflict between prayer and predetermination seemed as daunting a contradiction as that which Milton addresses in *Paradise Lost*: Why would an all-loving and all-knowing God allow man to fall in the

Garden of Eden and lose the gift of eternal life, eternal happiness? I had been teaching *Paradise Lost* for twenty-five years. I had not, however, really experienced the complexities of theology in that magnificent work first hand.

I was not discovering for the first time the seeming contradictory nature of Christianity; I was simply feeling the power of this contradiction because it had become for me more than an intellectual question. My life had become a lesson in the nature of God's love, and I was very much the student, by no means the teacher. I felt the need for resolution in order to really understand what had happened and was happening in my life. And I had three weeks to come up with something to share at church. At least my parents would be able to drive down from North Carolina to attend the service at which I was speaking, and visit with the members of my church family who had done so much for them while I was in the hospital.

So, what was I going to say to the people who had so completely embraced me and my family, whose prayers had begun the night I suffered the heart attack and had continued through my "miraculous" recovery? I use the word miraculous because it was so often used by those who had seen me collapse on the softball field. I particularly remember the haunted look in Jay Cooper's eyes when he told me that at one point Daryl, Geno, and Frank had thought they were feeling a pulse and then lost it. They feared that my heart had stopped yet again. Jay said that he and my teammates were praying for me, and that he looked up just as Daryl had said he had found a pulse. "I saw a miracle," Jay told me, "an answer to our prayers." I wasn't looking for a miracle after talking with Mike, just a little inspiration. It would have been out and out selfish to expect a second miracle so soon after the first.

I felt pretty comfortable when I stepped into the pulpit a few weeks later and said, "If you're going to have a heart attack, it is a pretty good idea to do it at a church-league softball game. You get on a lot of prayer lists." This was not just an effort at humor. I believed it, as I believed then and believe now that had that attack happened anywhere else, I would not have survived. Then I told the congregation that I did not have the wisdom to understand how it could be both God's plan, and at the same time an answer to prayer, that I survive. I simply had the faith that *in* God's plan these two seemingly contradictory realities do not conflict.

In the summer of 2001, I astonished a lot of people with my

fierce determination to survive. They astonished me much more with their even greater determination to help me do it. And to help me understand God's role in my life. What I gained then has remained with me as I have embraced my new life in EMS. In fact, I am often asked whether what happened to me in 2001 caused me after retiring from teaching to become an EMS worker.

The first time the question was posed, my response came quickly to mind. My response has never changed even slightly. Surviving sudden cardiac death had nothing to do with my deciding to become an EMS responder or to continue my training until I was a paramedic. It has had everything to do with *how* I do that job.

*****

EMS workers will tell you that the television version of what we do contrasts significantly with what being a paramedic actually involves. Most of our patients do not really need emergency treatment; many simply need a ride to the hospital. Some do not even "need" that. I have actually been dispatched to work on a broken telephone, or, as it turned out, a telephone that needed to be plugged in to a live electrical socket.

My wife avoids watching television shows with me that involve EMS because she grows weary of hearing me critique what we are watching. "It's a television show." Even if she doesn't say that exactly, I can feel her response to my shaking my head or mumbling something about "that's the wrong dose" or "you can still treat asystole."

Based on television, however, EMS workers weave in and out of heavy traffic with lights flashing and sirens screaming, jump out of their trucks at the ER and unload their patients in a flash, then rush their cots down ER hallways, breathlessly giving vital signs, reviewing treatment protocols they have followed, and directing some flirtatious comments at a nurse who makes a pair of scrubs look like an outfit she bought at Victoria's Secret. They are quickly surrounded by a large group of nurses and doctors, none of whom seem to have other patients, even though the ER is congested with activity. It is never like that—almost never.

After we loaded Sami and left for the hospital, Richard made the drive to the emergency room in twelve minutes. In the back, it had seemed much longer, but later when I was filling out my prehospital report and Dispatch gave me our times, I realized that to get us to the hospital so quickly, and not toss me around like a single potato in the bed of a wagon, Richard must have negotiated the traffic between the scene of the accident and the hospital with particular skill. We had been several miles out, though most of it, fortunately, by interstate.

The trauma team was waiting as we arrived, perhaps a dozen nurses, ER medics, and technicians. Because of the brevity of my radio report, they had little information about the arriving patient. They knew to expect a child, seriously injured in a MVC. That was enough. They were a quiet group as Richard and I wheeled our cot into the trauma room and moved Sami to the waiting bed. I scanned the faces of the team members. What showed in their stony expressions was the intense focus the challenge demanded. They had gathered in the primary trauma room, ready to do the job that had caused them to want to work in the ER to begin with. The team leader, a nurse named Rose, I did not know well. But I did know enough about Rose to realize that the team treating Sami was being led by an gifted nurse.

I repeated quickly what little I knew—how Sami had been injured in a high-speed collision; that she had been in a car seat; that she had been in the driver-side back seat, exactly where the primary impact had taken place; that she had been immobilized on scene. I then followed up with the longer list of what I had not been able to do in route because of having to suction to keep her airway open. I had not been able to bag her and had to rely on blow-by oxygen instead. I had not gained IV access. I had not been able to repeat my initial trauma assessment or take a second set of vitals.

I talked; the trauma team worked. Sami was placed beside a Broselow tape so that based on her height, proper drug dosages, proper ET tube size, and other crucial information for treating a child was at hand. Sami was no longer vomiting, so a respiratory therapist placed a mask over her mouth and nose and began to gently squeeze the blue bulb that would fill her lungs with oxygen. One of the ER medics took her tiny arm in his large hands, wrapped a blue tourniquet around her bicep, palpated a vein, and smoothly inserted a twenty gauge catheter into her left antecubital vein. With IV access in place and the ER doctor methodically giving orders, Rose sedated Sami and administered paralytics so that her gag reflex was suppressed and she could be intubated. Although she was a trauma patient, her respiratory effort was so weak that she required advanced airway management. With easy movements, the doctor slipped an ET tube into Sami's trachea and secured it with practiced skill. Finally, she could be ventilated and more efficiently receive the oxygen her body needed. Richard and I stood to the side and observed the ER staff do all those things that I had not been able to do in route as I would have wished.

The ER physician completed his assessment, ordered a quick set of x-rays that could be sent to the receiving hospital, and indicated that he wanted her prepared for immediate flight to a pediatric trauma center. That was when I learned that the MedFlight chopper that I had canceled had been redirected and was waiting to transport Sami to the trauma unit in Johnson City, Tennessee. The trip in a ground unit running hot would take forty-five minutes. The "bird" could get her there in ten. Sami needed that extra thirty-five minutes!

The flight medic was Earl Carter. Once again, as with having Rose as the trauma team leader, Sami's care was going to be transferred to one of the finest EMS workers I have met, one of those paramedics who wants the calls that matter. Earl pulled me aside. He wanted to know everything I could tell him about his patient. I had taken PHTLS (Prehospital Trauma Life Support) class with Earl and knew that he was asking me to be his eyes at the scene. The recording nurse on the trauma team joined us. Slowly, I tried to put the pieces together for Earl and the nurse, again struck by how much I was not able to tell them and how little I had been able to do in route. My frustration with how little I was able to actually accomplish must have been as obvious to them as it was to me.

"You got her here alive. She has a chance," Earl said.

Earl was particularly interested in my description of the accident scene. I was able to describe for him the twisted metal of the two cars where they had collided in exactly the way that placed most of the kinetic force against the side of the car where Sami had been sitting. I was able to tell him her condition on scene and describe my efforts to keep her airway open during transport. Earl's eyes focused as he took in the little information I could provide as if he were digesting, sorting, and preparing what he would be doing once his chopper was in route.

What I couldn't tell him or the recording nurse was Sami's name. Most of the events of that evening were clear to me. Somehow, however, I had managed to leave the scene without knowing her last name. Richard and I had been on scene only very briefly, and I was unable to pull from those moments anything except hearing another little girl who had been in the car, who turned out to be Sami's sister, as she asked me, "How is Sami?"

I was simply not able to put my brief conversations with the first responders or the moment of talking with Junior Musick together well enough to say whether I had ever heard her last name. I was unsettled by my not being able to come up with her name. I was completely clear on most of what had happened but in a dream-like daze about something as simple as her name. That sense that I was looking through a thick fog troubled me.

* * * * *

I awoke on a Thursday night, three weeks and a day after suffering sudden cardiac death on May 15, 2001. My older daughter Kimberly was in my room. My weakness and confusion kept me from really grasping exactly where I was or what had happened. Kimberly explained to me that I had "died" in the middle of a softball game three weeks earlier. She told me about how my friend Nancy had found her at work to tell her what had happened and then went to the emergency room with her. I asked Kimberly to dial Nancy's phone number. Nancy and I talked a moment, before I fell asleep. I told her thank you.

Nancy was one of the first of many people, as I would learn, who had given themselves to helping me and my family work our way through the struggles that we faced and to whom I would be giving my thanks.

The following morning, I continued to learn and understand exactly what had happened three weeks earlier. I had been the central character in a drama that led my cardiologist's assistant, Darby, to refer to me as a one in 10,000 patient. I may have been the main character, but it had been a drama with an extensive cast of supporting characters, a cast of extraordinary people.

The Thursday after I woke up I was visited by my parents and children, members of my softball team, friends who were able to gain access to the Cardiac Intensive Care unit, and Geno, a police officer and one of three men who performed CPR after I collapsed. The events that they helped me piece together, I do not remember at all. By seeing those events through their eyes, however, I am able to offer a reliable narrative.

Tuesday, May 15, 2001, I submitted my spring-semester final grades in time to go with my younger daughter Kate to her voice recital. Several family friends had attended, including my best friend Steve, who brought Kate a bouquet of roses. Steve and his wife had only just begun their family, and while they had been without children Kate had been the beneficiary of Steve's attention. He had sat with me at her gymnastics meets over the years and always made her feel a welcome part of our city-league softball team when she joined us in the dugout at our games. Kate was singing in what would be the first of many voice recitals. I know I was there, but do not remember anything about the evening.

After the recital, she attended a year-end banquet at school for the students involved in speech and debate activities. I had just enough time to get to the ballpark for the second game in my new team's double header. A knee injury had forced me to leave the independent league, but I was enjoying playing in the church league for the team from my new church, Aldersgate United Methodist. I arrived just in time to take the mound for the second game. In my haste, I had forgotten my knee brace but decided to play without it.

I was playing a good game; at least that is what I have been told. The opposing team had not scored, when I had my first at bat in the third inning. The catcher for the other team, Geno, taunted me at the plate about not giving him or his teammates anything to hit. I responded to his taunts by grounding out, for the third out of the inning. I tossed my bat and ran to the dugout where I grabbed my glove and ball and hustled to the mound.

With my first pitch, the game took a turn. Geno's teammate drove the ball to the fence. I dropped to the ground. Geno later told me that he thought I was just "goofing off" after our banter at the plate. The third baseman on my team knew better; Daryl ran to the mound. Frank, a park worker in the clubhouse watching the game, knew better; he dashed down the stairs and onto the field. Geno saw their reactions and rushed to the mound. They began the exhausting CPR procedures, while someone else called 911.

When he visited me in the hospital, Geno, a Montgomery police officer, told me about their efforts. He said that at one point he was sure that he had broken my ribs and found himself shouting, "You're not going to die on me!" He told me how several minutes into the resuscitation process, my stomach had distended, and I had vomited. He and Daryl rolled me to my side; Daryl swiped his fingers through my mouth to clear vomit from my airway and then resumed mouth-to-mouth ventilations. Anyone who has ever performed CPR knows that in a short time even three men can be exhausted by the physical effort required. They worked for twenty minutes, waiting for an ambulance.

Fain Field is a city softball complex in Montgomery with five fields and extensive warm-up areas. As the events on our field were relayed through the complex, the four other games stopped. Players from the other teams hustled over and joined my teammates in the outfield where they hit their knees. They were joined by the players from the teams waiting for the next games to begin. The outfield became an ocean of brightly colored jerseys with the names of churches throughout Montgomery emblazoned across their backs. Daryl, Geno, and Frank continued their efforts to give me a chance to live. Probably 300 softball players, most of them with no idea who I was, continued theirs as well—they prayed.

Since the night I woke up, I have been, am now, and shall ever be overwhelmed by the thought that so many people joined in one prayer, that I live, that it be God's will that I survive. That I knew almost none of them adds to my amazement, but then I hardly knew my teammates. A member of Aldersgate United Methodist church for only a few months, I had joined that church after twenty-five years of not attending services anywhere.

My life was out of control. I had to do something before my children began to suffer.

What would have happened if I had been anyplace other than on that softball field when my heart stopped? I was at the only place where I could survive an MI as serious as the one that stopped my heart. Proverbs 16: 9 says: "A man's mind plans his way, but the Lord directs his steps." I may have realized during the fall of 2000 that my life was out of control, but it was God who directed my steps to Aldersgate United Methodist Church, to a genuinely loving church family, and ultimately to Fain Field where I was in the company of capable people to provide CPR and loving people who would pray for my survival.

Before my finding my way to Aldersgate, at that time of night, I would have probably been in a bar, not on a softball field on church-league night. After my former wife died the previous August, I found myself trying to be a good father for two girls who had lost their mother. Initially my reaction to the struggle had been to use the time when my younger daughter, who was still living at home, was at a school function or staying with friends to drink and smoke myself into forgetfulness. I had almost managed to drink and smoke myself into the grave, leaving my children without either of their parents to love them through the difficult times and to share their joy during their triumphs.

Never Alone in the Back

*****

The dispatch was inevitable: "I need Rescue 3 to go to City Park, to the softball field. We have an unresponsive male patient who has collapsed on the pitcher's mound." The words, an echo that froze my thoughts, seemed not possible. But I was the ALS provider on Rescue 3.

As my partner Jacob and I moved to the ambulance, the fire lieutenant on duty said, "If you need us, call."

Behind him, Mark and Tracy stopped in their tracks. They knew, Mark especially. His eyes were frozen and lines creased his forehead. He understood. A skilled paramedic, Mark had been my teacher. He had become my friend, and he knew very well the irony that I would receive this call. But he wasn't the duty officer. It wasn't his decision whether the engine would run this EMS call.

Jacob and I ran hot. The park was only about a mile from the station. Behind the park entrance, the ball field was illuminated by banks of lights. A large group of players had gathered around the pitcher's mound. Some of the players opened the gate in the corner of left field and waved to us. Jacob eased the ambulance through the gate and across the outfield grass to the dirt infield. I jumped out and made my way to the mound.

Lying in the dirt, sweating profusely, his body drawn up, lay a young man, his hands clutching at his chest. His wife squatted beside him, her hand brushing at his hair. His teammates and the members of the other team surrounded them.

He was awake, the first good news of the evening. Jacob had unloaded and was bringing the stretcher. As I cut away my patient's jersey, I gathered the information I needed. Name: Martin. Age: 39. Medical history: None. Pain on a scale of 1-10: 10. Substernal pain radiating to his left arm. We needed him in the truck. And as I voiced that thought, hands appeared all around me. Loving hands. "Whatever you need," a strong voice said. And that quickly, Martin was secured to the cot and loaded.

Before I could climb in his wife took my arm. Her hand fought to remain steady. "I'm Martin's wife. Is he . . .?" She choked on her tears.

"Let me see what we have. You can ride in the front with us if you like."

By the time I climbed up, Jacob had placed Martin on high-flow oxygen and the cardiac monitor and started collecting a set of vital signs. Jacob was an EMT-Basic. We had never ridden together before that night. But he knew what to do in the back of an ambulance.

Martin's EKG showed a second-degree, type 1 AV block. It displayed ST elevation, a clear indication of an ongoing heart attack. We were not using 12-lead EKGs in the field at that point, but I did not need a 12-lead EKG or doctor to help me see what was happening. The rhythm was textbook clear and potentially lethal. Martin presented with all the signs and symptoms indicating a heart attack. He would need rapid transport to a cath lab. We needed to go.

"His BP is 89/56," Jacob said as I studied the monitor. "His O_2 SAT is 92."

"Run it hot," I said.

"Is he okay?" Martin's wife shouted from the front.

"We need to get to the hospital," I responded as Jacob slipped out the door and dashed around to the driver's seat. "I am going to see if I can do something to help him with the pain. We'll go from there."

I would have loved to use one of those good television lines: "Absolutely, nobody dies in my truck!" And then give her a reassuring wink. The reality was that Martin's EKG revealed a dangerous heart dysrhythmia and evidence of ongoing cardiac muscle death. Without definitive treatment, his condition could deteriorate in the next minute. In 10 minutes. Maybe longer. Nothing that I could do would change the ultimate outcome. I could not truthfully say anything more reassuring to his wife, because I simply did not know what was going to happen while we were in route to the ER.

Martin's condition was serious, and I had limited options to help. I gave him 324 mg of aspirin, hoping that it would prevent any further platelet coagulation such as had created the existing block. Easing his pain would take some of the stress off his heart and reduce its demand for oxygen, thus reducing its workload. Lessening the workload on his heart would leave more oxygen for the not-yet-damaged muscle. However, his blood pressure was too low to administer nitroglycerin or even give morphine. I could not administer either drug without violating cardiac protocols. The ER doctor would not order it during transport given Martin's vital signs. Either would have helped his pain, but both could drop his already low blood pressure to a dangerous level.

As Jacob eased the ambulance off the field and began a rapid lights-and-sirens, transport, I had just a moment to glance out the back of the truck to see Martin's teammates gathered on the field--in prayer! I saw in them what I have so often imagined in my mind had occurred the night I collapsed--an outfield full of my teammates and other players praying for me.

In route I was able to start an 18 gauge IV in Martin's left anticubital vein. When Martin saw me pull out the supplies to start the IV, he asked, "Do you have to do that while we're moving?" Even through his pain, his fear of needles surfaced.

Martin's implied complaint caused me to hear in the back of my mind my EMS teachers stressing that we be able to function in route: "If you can't hit an IV in a moving truck, you don't need to be back there."

"It will be quick," I told Martin. And it was. I bolused fluids as rapidly as I could until I had a systolic blood pressure of 114. At that point I was able to give him a dose of nitro. However, I had been unable to do anything more, and Martin was still suffering significant pain as we arrived. I alerted the ER of my patient's condition and prepared him for external pacing just in case his condition deteriorated, although we were too close to the hospital to begin electrical therapy if his condition did not change for the worse.

Jacob and I moved Martin into a treatment room. I gave my report to the team leader, Bryan. A second nurse hooked Martin to a 12-lead EKG. The monitor confirmed what I had already seen on our 5-lead EKG in the truck. The ER doctor arrived as Jacob and I were leaving.

Martin's wife grabbed my arm. "Is he going to be okay?"

"I'm not the doctor, but I think there's a good chance he's having a heart attack."

"But he's only thirty-nine, "she whispered through her tears.

"I know," I said. "I had one at forty-seven. In fact, my heart stopped. On a pitcher's mound. Church-league night. And I'm here."

Her eyes widened as the significance of the coincidence sank in. She nodded and slipped back into Martin's room.

Before I had turned in my paperwork, Martin was on his way to the cath lab. Our response time had been good. He was young and strong. He'd had an MI at an early age, but his prospects for recovery were excellent.

I was angry that the lieutenant had not responded with us to the call. My patient would have benefitted from Mark's help in route. Already, however, I had learned that my strength as a medic lies in God. And as is so often the case for me, I find in Proverbs the words to keep this truth in my mind: "If you faint in the day of adversity, your strength is small." This passage means to me that if we forget that our strength lies in God, then our strength is indeed insignificant. If, however, we keep in mind that we are the instruments of God, if we strive to be the instruments He deserves, then we will have the ability we need to meet any challenge we face.

With this call, the parallels with my own experience tempted me to be weak, to let fear control my actions. Fortunately, my emotions about the similarities between the call and my own experience did not surface to interfere with my doing my job. They waited until I was leaving the hospital and then twisted a knot in my stomach until I reclaimed the picture of Martin's teammates and was reminded of the men with whom I played ball, of the blessing that Martin and I shared being part of a church-league softball team. Ultimately I was struck by the "rightness" in this call being mine, for I, perhaps more than anyone else, could reassure Martin's wife that she had reason to feel hope.

In that call, I found something precious. It created a vivid picture about my life that I had to this point only been able to experience through the words of others. Seeing Martin's teammates holding him in their hearts and prayers, ready to do anything I asked to help me treat him, I saw Daryl, Geno, Frank, Jay, and all the others who had given me my second life years earlier. A call that could have frozen me with memories or left me with sadness gave me an experience that lifted my heart. That call, which initially made me feel reticent, proved to be a gift from God. I praise Him for sending me to City Park to treat Martin that spring night!

*****

Not only did I not really know my teammates on my new softball team, they did not know much about me either. I was playing my first season with the team, and we were early in the spring schedule. I had been surprised at how quickly they had welcomed me, particularly as I was a pitcher and to make room on the team, Coach French Salter had been forced to move the player who had been pitching for several years to third base. The player who had needed to switch positions, Daryl Powell, had welcomed me to the team as enthusiastically as anyone and, ironically, had been the first person to realize something was wrong when I collapsed on the mound. He was the first person to initiate CPR.

Even though we were at this point in our lives playing church-league softball, most of us had enjoyed more competitive athletics. My new teammates appreciated my devil-may-care approach to competition--diving for ground balls, sliding into bases, and maintaining my quick reflexes that have always allowed me to snag line drives when I am pitching, especially those coming toward my head! At age forty-seven, and after several surgeries and broken bones as a result of sports injuries, I probably had no business at that point playing the game like a youngster. That, however, was how I played and enjoyed the game.

A torn ACL and LCL in my left knee had reduced me two years before to very limited mobility. I had hyper-extended my left leg stretching to beat a throw to first base. When my foot hit the base, my leg collapsed, and a snapping sound spoke of a serious injury. The second baseman on my team was a sports trainer who later confirmed my suspicions and arranged the next morning for me to see an orthopedic surgeon. Without ligaments in my knee, the joint was so loose that it felt ready to collapse with every step. However, that season my independent-league team had an excellent shot at winning our division, so I spent the rest of the spring and summer wrapping my knee tightly, hobbling instead of running, and continuing to pitch. My friend Steve and I had built that team over four years, and I was not letting an injury stop us from competing for lack of a pitcher. We won the division and took home the trophy. A few weeks later, I had surgery, which replaced the torn ligaments with a tendon graft. I would be able to play again, but at a pace that would not allow me another season in the independent league. When I joined Aldersgate United Methodist Church and again had an opportunity to compete, I jumped at the chance.

For the past two years, I had missed the arrival of spring practice, which in Alabama begins in February. I hungered for the rich aroma of new grass in the outfield and the feel of a well-groomed infield under my feet. I had missed the smell of a well-oiled glove. I was ready to play!

I felt good to be on a team again. In time I would get to know my teammates and enjoy their companionship as I had with the players on my previous team. A few things were different. I had never prayed before a game, never heard shouted reminders, "Hey this is church league," when an utterance from a player more appropriate to previous days in athletics slipped out. The irony was not lost on me; my previous team had been sponsored by a Montgomery pub, which had served as our gathering place after practices and games.

After I collapsed, and with all that was taking place as Daryl, Geno, and Frank continued CPR, one of my teammates, Press, asked if anyone knew whom to call to get in touch with my family. Only Press's wife, Donna, who worked with my friend Nancy, could come up with an option. Press remained near me on the field and called Donna who was sitting in the stands. Donna called Nancy. Through this cell-phone relay system, Press told Donna, who then told Nancy, what he was able to observe. They continued to relay messages until the ambulance arrived, at which point Nancy, who knew that my daughter Kimberly worked at Outback Steakhouse left to find her. Nancy also knew that my former wife, my children's mother, had died the previous August, and she accepted the job of telling one of them that their father might well be dying.

As I have had several years now to think about the inherent goodness and strength of a person who is willing to assume that responsibility, I have only been able to conclude that in Nancy lay that special kind of strength that does not back away from the difficult moments in life. Since becoming an EMS provider, one of the things that I have had to learn is to give terrible news to grieving family members. It is part of the job. I learned a lot about doing that job, however, from Nancy, who did it not out of obligation to a career, but out of a commitment and ability to do what was right.

*****

Working as a paramedic has taught me to respect the work of volunteers. Collapsing on a softball field and having new friends and teammates take me and my children into their hearts allowed me to see that the goodness of people comes not from long-established relationships, but rather from loving hearts. On many scenes to which I have responded, I have seen the same commitment to doing what is right from bystanders who do more than voice the Golden Rule, they live it!

My partner Kacy and I began a Friday shift by responding to a "seizure" call, only to find ourselves working a cardiac arrest which we and firefighter first responders worked aggressively and successfully. In route our patient regained a pulse. The rest of the shift proved rather uneventful, until, as we were returning from a public service call, we were dispatched to a strip mall parking lot where bystanders had called 911 to report a male sitting in his car in the parking lot of a strip mall having trouble breathing. We received the call a short distance from the scene but ran lights and sirens nonetheless. We arrived to find several men waving us to the location of the car where a young woman, perhaps ninety pounds, mostly arms, legs, and long brown hair, straddled the patient sitting in the driver's seat. The muscles in her legs were tight as guitar strings as she tried to balance herself. The steering wheel served as a seat. Her arms were pumping hard and fast as she attempted to do chest compressions. The car was rocking from her efforts. She was, as EMS providers say, "wearing it out!"

Given the position she and the patient were in, her efforts were of no real medical value; she had certainly not had CPR training, or else she would have known to move the patient to a hard surface.

What should matter, however, is not what she was not accomplishing, but rather what she was trying to accomplish. She was working as hard as anyone I have ever seen to assist a total stranger. As Kacy pulled the ambulance to a stop, I jumped out and ran to the patient. The young woman stepped back, panting, exhausted. Sweat dripped from her nose and chin. Her long brown hair was matted to her flushed cheeks. The outside temperature was in the mid-nineties, and CPR can exhaust a well-conditioned person in just a couple of minutes. She gladly gave up her position. I slipped into the car, pushed my hands under the patient's arm pits, and clasped his forearms to pull him out. A stout black man with shaved head and muscled arms stepped in. "How can I help?"

"Grab his legs as I slide him out."

Together, we eased our patient onto the long board that Kacy had brought and laid onto the pavement. I began chest compressions. Our patient looked to be in his late sixties, maybe seventies. His ribs cracked with the first compression. Kacy returned to the truck to get our cardiac monitor and airways equipment. Firefighters arrived on the scene to assist with the resuscitative efforts. Moments later, the girl who had been doing chest compressions when we arrived squatted next to me and said, "No one in the store knows who he is. What can I do?"

I looked into her brown eyes and said, "You did great. Thanks." I had to smile that as soon as she had been relieved from doing chest compressions she'd had the presence of mind to try to keep helping by identifying our patient for us. She brushed strands of hair from her eyes and stood back to watch as we intubated our patient and then moved him to the cot.

We were only minutes from the hospital. Usually, I like to work a cardiac arrest on scene for several minutes. An advanced life support truck is equipped and paramedics have the skills to do essentially anything an ER team can do for the first twenty minutes of treating a cardiac arrest. Three firefighters had responded, one a paramedic, so Kacy and I had the help we needed. Being so close to the hospital, however, I decided to remain on scene briefly, only long enough to intubate and confirm proper placement of the intubation tube, establish IV access, and give the first round of cardiac drugs. We transported emergency, with lights and sirens, leaving a gathering of citizen first responders and one exhausted young woman behind. When we arrived at the ER five or six minutes later, I gave my report to the doctor, including telling him that the patient had received on-scene CPR from a bystander. He assessed what we had done, examined the patient, told his team to halt resuscitation efforts, and declared the patient dead. His decision was an indirect compliment. We had done our job well. Nothing was left to do for the patient. Part of that compliment belonged to the young woman who first initiated treatment.

On scene, with a patient who had gone into cardiac arrest in a warm car on a hot day, many of the signs about how long he might have been down were masked by body warmth provided by environmental conditions. Probably, when the young woman initiated CPR, he had already been dead too long for even an experienced emergency responder to make a difference in the outcome. Again, however, the negative outcome for the patient speaks nothing about the wonderfully positive gift of her caring enough for a stranger to try to help. The widow who was notified by the police that her husband had passed away may never know of the love gift she and her husband had received. The young woman, and the other bystanders who guided us to the scene and stood at the ready as Kacy, the firefighters, and I took over treatment, were not featured later that evening on the local news. We hear regularly about those situations where bystanders have not responded when they have witnessed an emergency, an act of violence, or some other crisis. We rarely hear the opposite stories, the ones that feature one of God's children acting out of love to help a stranger as He taught us we should love one another through His son Jesus. I saw that love in the face of a petite young woman, dripping with sweat, long strands of damp hair covering her eyes and matted to her face, her arms windmilling as she tried to perform CPR chest compressions. God saw that love also, and surely He smiled! God may have called one of his children home from that strip mall parking lot that day, but several others of his children in that same lot, one a tiny woman with a huge heart, showed the rest of us what God calls on all of us to do while we are still of this world, to love and care for one another, to "do unto others . . ."

Chapter Three

Sami Musick was not the first child whom I had been dispatched to treat. The first had come a few weeks after my joining the Lifesaving Crew. Dispatch had indicated that the patient was an infant with difficulty breathing. We did not have a specific age, and difficulty breathing in a child could mean anything from a stuffy nose, to croup, to a serious pulmonary condition. My stomach tightened as my partner and I pulled away from the station to respond to a pediatric call, but nothing in the dispatch was, on the surface, overly concerning. Except that the patient was a baby! My partner and I ran the call emergency, and, as our local protocols require with any difficulty breathing call, Dispatch sent a fire unit to assist.

Our dispatch address indicated a neighborhood of lower-income families, families with limited education, possibly a patient whose mother had received little prenatal attention before giving birth and few if any visits to a pediatrician after the delivery for regular medical checkups. Possibly, these assumptions would all prove inaccurate, but after a while those of us who work in EMS begin to know our regular patients and the areas in which we run calls. The demographics of healthcare are like the demographics of crime, business opportunities, or any other social issue; they tend to be reliable and helpful, especially while trying to anticipate what to expect and how to prepare a treatment plan while in route. Our patient, on this occasion, was a child who might very well be found in a crack house. Were definitely responding to an area where the use of drugs was widespread. This fact provided yet another in-route consideration for what my partner, Brandon, and I might find when we arrived. For that reason and because the patient was a child, I asked Dispatch to send law enforcement to the scene as well.

Brandon and I arrived just ahead of the fire unit and police cruiser. The address proved to be an apartment in an old, three-story frame house, its white paint peeled away or faded out. The roof sagged and was covered by old tar shingles that were cracked or missing altogether. The front yard was over-grown and cluttered with broken toys, neglected flower pots, and various other characteristic signs of a life lived with little hope or ambition. Trash bags, piled high along the sidewalk, forced us to park about half a block away in order for the fire truck to have room to park as well.

A crowd had gathered on the front porch of the house. They were the predictable neighborhood on-lookers who found the arrival of emergency-response units often signaled a bit of entertainment, so their presence did not indicate anything unusual. Thank goodness I had called for law enforcement, if for no other reason than we would have officers to keep these people out of the way while we attended to our patient.

Nothing about the crowd seemed threatening, however, so Brandon and I did not wait for the officers to arrive. The scene appeared safe. If anything, as we approached, the people on the porch were quieter than usual, certainly not aggressive or threatening. Their quiet behavior troubled me. It was, in fact, so much not the norm that we might well be facing a more serious situation than I had realized based on the sketchy information Dispatch had been able to offer.

"Let's get on in there," I whispered to Brandon.

As we worked our way through the crowd of seven or eight people milling about on the porch, I noticed one was what we call a frequent flyer. She suffered from COPD and regularly called 911 to be taken to the hospital. She had always been a frustrating patient as the best treatment plan for her would be to quit smoking and use her oxygen, not make a run to the hospital in an ambulance every few days. I almost expected her to ask us to take a look at her, and when she didn't I had my second indication that we needed to get to our patient. I was right.

We walked through the door of a dirty, cluttered apartment to find a woman, probably in her forties and a young girl in tears. The older woman was holding her, stroking her matted blonde hair, and whispering quietly. My gaze, however, was immediately drawn across the room. On the sofa, propped against throw pillows was a baby, three or maybe four weeks old. I could tell without taking a step our patient's condition.

"Take them to the kitchen," I said to Brandon, nodding to an open door on the other side of the entry room and handing him the clipboard with our prehospital report form. "Get the basics."

As he directed the two women out of the front room, the fire medic, Sean, came in behind us.

"Oh, God," he whispered.

The baby on the sofa had been dead much too long to consider resuscitation efforts. Her mouth and eyes were open. Her skin was blue, and rigor mortis had set in. I did not need a second medic on scene to conclude that the condition did not indicate medical response. I did, however, welcome Sean's presence, AND that of the officers. My job had become not to try to keep a patient alive, but rather to tell a teenage mother that her daughter was dead.

Sean called the ER that monitors all EMS radio traffic to tell the radio-room attendants that we would not be transporting a patient. The officer called Dispatch to initiate the investigation process, which would begin immediately. I covered the infant with a sheet and stepped into the kitchen where Brandon was quietly getting the basic information.

"Please," the girl pleaded, "I just want my baby back." Tears streamed down her gaunt face, and her thin arms dangled limp at her sides. Her body sagged as if at any moment she would drop to the floor. Brandon managed to get her into a kitchen chair.

"I'm sorry," I said, holding her gaze. "Your baby has died. There's nothing we can do for her."

She slumped further into the chair, looking at no one. Just repeating, "All I want is my baby back. Please, I just want my baby back."

I worked with the police for about thirty minutes while Sean checked the mother's medical condition to be sure that she was in no immediate danger. The despair, which had stripped her strength and crushed her spirit, made her condition potentially dangerous.

What we discovered was that the eighteen-year-old mother had brought her baby to her bed during the night and then, apparently, in her sleep rolled on top of her. When she awoke and found her child lifeless she had carried her to the sofa to try to wake her up. Then she called 911. The police would have to conduct a full investigation, but the facts appeared pretty obvious. During all this, the neighbor I had noticed as one of our regulars had come to the apartment and was doing a wonderful job of holding and trying to comfort the young mother while the lady who had first been with her talked with the police. I felt guilty about my earlier thoughts concerning her. On this day, she displayed only concern for another person.

The call had required me for the first time not only to tell a family that their loved one had died, but to do so when the patient was a child and the mother, a child herself, who had been the cause of her baby's death. As a Christian, my impulse was to try to offer comfort and to do so by referring to God's love, to say something to indicate that a child, with all its innocence, had already been blessed to find a place in Heaven in God's loving care. However, as an EMS professional I do not have this option. Not knowing my patients or the circumstances of the families, I have to accept that any mention of religion has risks. Such words could actually inflame an already combustive situation. James 1:22 says, "be doers of the word." My ability to act as a Christian on this occasion lay in the manner of my talking with the child's mother. What she was facing was a fact none of us could change. Her child was gone. My job was to tell her and do so in such a way as to not obscure with my words that her child was dead.

As much as my heart might have wished to say more, to say what she had to hear in a less direct way, my job as a professional and, I think, as a Christian could only be completed with direct honesty. Only in that way could I be a "doer of the word."

I find, however, that situations such as this call presented, acting as a Christian is in fact easier than thinking as one. To say that God is present in the home where a child has died is a challenge; to find God in such a home is a far greater challenge. By the time I responded to the car wreck in which Sami Musick was injured, I had gained enough EMS experience to recognize God's presence in horrible situations. But seeing God in the blue-tinted face of a baby accidentally smothered by her mother requires a faith that does demand as a prerequisite a palpable and comprehendible justice, the kind that enabled Abraham to embrace the command that he sacrifice his son Isaac in order to prove his love for and obedience to God. Our reaction, however, to such loss as that felt by an eighteen-year-old mother who has accidentally smothered her own child is to try to brace against our grief and not see God's presence. Only by faith would it be possible to find God in such settings. Intellectually, we will not find God's presence in many of the horrible events that we see and especially in those which we directly experience. If we try to build our Christianity on thought alone and disregard faith, we will be, as Jesus explained, like the "foolish man who built his house upon the sand" (Matthew 7: 26). And yet, faith strong enough to lose a child, and yet believe; faith such as the Musick family found as they struggled first with the question of Sami's survival and then the months of treatment and therapy; is a faith that is precious and hard won. It is a faith that ultimately requires prayer to find and prayer to keep. C. S. Lewsi, said, "There are two kinds of people: those who say to God, 'Thy will be done,' and who say, 'All right, then, have it your way.'" The kind of faith that the Musick family demonstrated led them in their prayers to what Lewis characterized as accepting God's way, not accepting that God will have His way.

*****

After returning to the station the night Sami was injured, I called my wife. She, in ways far beyond me, embodies the capacity for Christian faith. We had joined a church in our new community in North Carolina. Partly because of my working so often on Sundays and partly because I continued to struggle with losing my home church at Aldersgate, I had not really involved myself. She, on the other hand, had thrown herself into the life of our church.

When I called her and told her about Sami, she began to pray that night. She took with her to church the next day our request for prayer for Sami and her family. Not many days passed before Sami's story appeared on an Internet site devoted to critical patients, offering updates on their conditions and in Sami's case, requesting prayer. Her parents were doing everything they could to secure for her the medical treatment that her condition required, including, ultimately, moving her to a specialized pediatric rehabilitation facility. They also, however, sought the healing of God and asked that the community of believers to which they belonged join them in prayer. The trauma team nurse, Rose, who had done such a skillful job with Sami, told me about the web page, and I visited it often during the weeks that followed. I was struck by the pictures of Sami, those which showed her playing t-ball and holding a giant piece of birthday cake with red icing, taken before her injury, as well as those taken after that showed her with her left eye lid sagging, the left side of her face drooped, her left arm limp. And, as the family asked, I prayed for her and for them. And I thought again, as I had after my own crisis, about the act of prayer and the role it plays in our lives.

* * * * *

The Bible teaches Christians extensively about the practice of prayer--how to pray, the power of prayer, the role of prayer in worship. Probably the most significant of the Biblical passages on prayer comes from Matthew 6: 5-15, in which Jesus speaks of the importance of quiet prayer, prayer which allows the individual to communicate intimately with God. Jesus then provides the example of how to pray in the form of what we now refer to as The Lord's Prayer. We repeat those words so often during public worship that we might well forget that Jesus indicated before providing this example of prayer that his followers should pray in private: "But when you pray, go into your room and shut the door and pray to your Father who is in secret, and your Father who sees in secret will reward you" (Matthew 6: 6). We can learn much about the nature of prayer from this brief verse, that prayer should be an intimate communication between man and God and that God responds to prayers thus delivered. In The Lord's Prayer itself, moreover, we can learn much by example.

The Lord's Prayer divides neatly into three parts, the first which honors God, the second which asks that His "will be done," and the third which makes requests of God. For most of us, the third of these three often becomes the sole purpose of prayer. The Bible even encourages us to pray for God's intercession during times of difficulty by narrating numerous events when those who followed God in the Old Testament and his Son in the New Testament were persecuted and then, after praying, were delivered by God's intervention. Sunday worship in Christian churches typically includes a time for the congregation to offer their prayer requests, and many churches, including Aldersgate United Methodist, have a prayer group that meets regularly to seek God's blessings for those in need. These prayer warriors find in Acts 12: 5, in the story of how Peter was imprisoned by Herod, the example to follow: "So Peter was kept in prison; but earnest prayer for him was made to God by the church." The prayers of the church were rewarded when God sent angels to deliver Peter.

Both in my experience with prayer during my own health crisis and in my experience in EMS, I must confess that the focus of prayer has been occupied with asking God's intervention in my life or in the lives of those for whom I have prayed. After I was released from the hospital in 2001, I learned not only how my teammates and players from other teams had prayed for me during the efforts to resuscitate me, but also how churches throughout the city had added me to their prayer lists, often before they even had my name. They prayed for me and for my family. The very public nature of my crisis had captured the hearts of people I did not know and only a few of whom I have since met. "Oh, you're the guy we prayed for . . ." was a not an uncommon statement when I would meet someone new at the health club or in some other gathering.

Sami Musick's family, when they were able to offer her story on an internet site devoted to people facing health crises, sought the prayers of others, of strangers who, like them, believed that through prayer Sami would be healed. Prayer became for them, as it does for so many, the instrument that kept them from otherwise feeling hopeless. As I read the comments others made on that website and saw the community of Christians turn their prayers to God on behalf of Sami, I remembered well my own experience with the contradiction between God's having a divine plan for us all and His answering prayer. I addressed this seeming conflict when speaking to my church back in Montgomery simply by saying that somehow in God's plan what appears to us to be a conflict must be only an appearance, not a reality. Now, having twice experienced the power of prayer and the desire to receive prayer through two different but very personal and very dramatic experiences, I feel God has allowed me to better understand prayer than I did in 2001. Above all else, prayer is the ultimate act of faith. When we pray, more than at any other time, we become aware that by faith we have accepted the reality of God, of His presence in our lives, even though we cannot see or touch Him. When we pray during times of crisis, we place our trust in God's ability to intervene in our lives in ways that others whom we can see and touch cannot. Though we cannot empirically experience God, through faith we accept that He can do more to heal than can the doctors with whom we can speak, who are "real" in our lives. Through faith, expressed by our turning to God in prayer, especially during times when we are most fearful, we are saying that His unseen power is the ultimate power in all things. And when we pray for an outcome that does not occur, our faith is even more profoundly tested to continue to believe not only in God's power, but in His goodness as well.

And yet, the Christian who has prayed for what was not given but whose faith remains intact, who turns to God yet again when faced with another crisis, is the Christian whom we admire. Such a Christian, the one who has suffered as Job suffered, and yet who continues to love God and to trust God, as Job loved and trusted God, is the Christian who provides us a lesson in faith and who demonstrates for us the true meaning of prayer.

Prayer, however, does more than express our faith; it strengthens us by giving us a sense of control in those situations which seem beyond our control. When I found myself thinking about how my surviving a massive heart attack confirmed for some people the power of prayer, and for others the fact that God has a life plan for all of us, my academic mind stirred. It caused me to genuinely struggle with what I could only view as a contradiction. The question seemed simple: Why go to God in prayer with our requests, when the outcome of all crises exists in the mind of God before we even take our requests to Him? What, then, is the value of prayer?

As I have watched my patients, and especially the family and friends of my patients, pray, I have realized that through prayer we are seeking God's mercy, but we are also saying that even in the most horrific of circumstances we have a sense of control over what happens in our lives. Prayer is the gift God gives us so that no matter what happens, we are not enslaved by our human limitations. Prayer is certainly an act of faith, an expression in our belief in God and our trust that God cares what happens to us. Through prayer we acknowledge that a power greater than our own, and greater than the seemingly random forces of an earthly life, will set the path of our lives.

However, prayer is more. Prayer becomes, with our faith, a powerful weapon that allows us not to feel helpless. Sami Musick's parents understood this when they turned to prayer. Her mother, though a nurse, recognized that to be saved and healed Sami needed medical treatment beyond her training and ability, beyond that of the nurses and doctors at the ER, certainly beyond any skills I possessed. But not beyond God's skills. I felt the same sense of helplessness while transporting Sami. I was able to offer little that she needed but was keenly aware that in God's hands she would be fine. So, I prayed for her. I prayed that what I was able to do, I would do well. I also prayed that God would hold her in His care.

When I collapsed on the softball field, much the same occurred. Daryl, Frank, and Geno used their hands to do what man can do. However, my teammates and all the players and their families participated just as directly in the efforts to save my life. By praying, they became involved. They defeated any sense of helplessness by doing that which is most important in any crisis--turning it over to God. Ironically, when we face a crisis by "turning it over to God," we are in fact not releasing our control; we are exerting it. Through prayer we are not saying we have nothing to offer, we are offering the greatest of the strengths that God allows us—our faith.

As an EMS provider, I feel that prayer is important. The fact that I pray does not free me from my obligation to train, to learn, to improve. Asking that God be with me and with my patients does not become a substitute for diligence. If I am going to ask God through prayer to guide my thoughts and direct my hands, I feel particularly obligated to give Him the best-trained mind and the most skillful hands for His use as my dedication and study can provide. If I am going to pray to be His instrument, I feel compelled to provide Him as effective an instrument as possible. Prayer and faith are not a substitute for taking responsibility. Prayer and faith provide the spiritual context within which we can become responsible servants to God.

My teammates prayed for me as I lay on the softball field. Their prayers found answer. What occurred in the next hour or so was that God placed in my path exactly the right people to take up the challenge of keeping me alive as my care was transferred from one person to the next, from Daryl, Frank, and Geno to the paramedics and then to ER teams who received me, and the specialists who gave me back my life.

*****

Since becoming an ALS provider, I have worked only ten cardiac arrests. I have been the AIC, attendant in charge, for eight of these. Of the ten, only six have I and my partners "gotten back." Of those six, only three left the ER for a room on the floor. All three died within days.

That I was brought back proved surprising. That I left the hospital weeks later, startling. That I have been able to return to a normal life--a life that includes playing softball, seeing both my daughters graduate from college, finding a second chance at living a full personal life with my wife JeDonne--is miraculous. The miracle began with Daryl, Frank, and Geno performing CPR, extended to my teammates hitting their knees in prayer, and continued with the EMS team that treated me on scene. What I have learned about their efforts, now with the knowledge I have about the options a paramedic has when working a cardiac arrest, makes me appreciate how fortunate I was to receive that chain of care.

The paramedics who treated me found a pulse, but also a dangerous cardiac dysrhythmia. They found my respiratory effort inadequate. Therefore, before even leaving the scene they intubated me and provided assisted ventilation, while at the same time blocking my esophagus so that if I aspirated again my lungs would be protected from the vomitus. They established IV access. They then shocked my heart using synchronized cardioversion techniques in an effort to convert my dysrhythmia to a perfusing rhythm, one which would generate adequate heart activity to circulate oxygen to my body. Then, they loaded me for emergency transport to the closest ER.

At the time, Montgomery had three hospitals. The one closest to Fain Field was the most limited; however, EMS protocols dictated then, as they do now, that the paramedics take me to the nearest hospital should my condition become unstable. At that hospital, the ER doctors basically confirmed the excellent prehospital care I had received, found that my condition would allow them to remove the intubation tube so that the EMS crew did not have to continue "bagging" me, and prepared me for transport to the level 1 trauma center where a cardiologist would assume my care.

As soon as the ambulance had left the softball complex, Press and Donna had told Nancy where I was being taken. She left to find Kimberly at the steak house. Kimberly then called her aunt Tami, my former sister-in-law, who had been at Kate's recital and knew to look for her at school. Kimberly and Nancy arrived at the ER just as I was being moved to the ambulance for transfer to the next hospital. Although I have no memory of these events, Kimberly has told me that when she arrived I awoke for a moment, recognized her, and said, "I'm sorry," before then falling back into unconsciousness, which lasted for three weeks.

Kimberly again contacted her aunt and told her that I was being moved. Tami had found Kate, so they rerouted to the trauma center. They were at the ER when the ambulance bringing me arrived. Kate's friends from school, who had also been at the banquet, as well as her teacher Mrs. Coodey and her husband, rushed to the emergency room to be with her.

The ER hallways were filled by the time the ambulance arrived to transfer my care; however, the admitting staff needed Kimberly, my one available relative over age eighteen, to sign paperwork approving my treatment. Kimberly was the one person who had not yet arrived. Kate, who had been through so many similar episodes during her mother's struggle with and death from cancer, knew this routine. She understood standing along a hospital corridor or sitting in a waiting room for news about a parent. She had held up the first time. However, the stress of the situation, the questions about what she should do overwhelmed her—the one-two punch life had thrown her tested her strength. Mrs. Coodey's husband took control of the scene.

"I'm Judge Coodey," he told the ER staff. "What do you need signed?" Once again, God had placed in my path exactly the person who had the ability to give shape to His will. Judge Coodey was able, in his capacity as a judge, to authorize any actions the doctors deemed necessary without family approval. No ER would have denied me treatment without signatures on the admission papers. What Judge Coodey was able to do, however, was calm the moment for Kate's sake. He--my teammates at the softball complex, the paramedics, Nancy, Tami, Kate's friends and teacher—they all had accepted the unique roles that God had written for them. They had all accepted those roles readily and performed them with love. And this cast of very special, gifted, and loving players was about to be joined by one of the most skilled doctors to ever cross my path, the trauma-center cardiologist, Dr. Ahmed.

*****

God's earthly servants appear in many forms. They make themselves known during a variety of situations. Many appear to be at the right place at the right time, as with Judge Coodey, but then readily take advantage of that location and time to serve God and his children. Others, like the young woman who began CPR on a cardiac arrest patient in a strip mall parking lot, thrust themselves into an emergency situation because they understand and embrace doing the right thing. They teach us not to judge each other by who we are or how we look, but rather by what we are—what we do.

Perhaps the most unlikely-looking of God's servants I know is paramedic P.J. Fleenor. His is a short, stout country boy, a farmer, a firefighter with the Fire Department, and a paramedic with the Lifesaving Crew. He looks, to use the language of the region, as "rough as a cob." His shoulders rise up into his head without the interruption of a neck. Red bristles, like those on a bottle brush, spring from his head. His fingers are short; several have been broken during farm accidents so that they are knotted and bent. He sweats with the slightest exertion, even on cold days. I have seen him arrive at work and have to wash the manure from his boots because he has come straight from the feed lot.

Firehouse humor being what it is, P.J.'s physique has earned him such nicknames as "walking small," "paramidget" and "Little Ennis," a reference for those who are familiar with Burt Reynolds' classic *Smokey and the Bandit*. No matter his appearance, nor the jokes that he endures, P.J. is not only the most gifted paramedic I know; he also has an amazing knack for keeping life in perspective. "Things" just seem to happen to P.J. that happen to no one else. He takes life in stride, just as he smiles and brushes aside the taunts from his fellow firefighters about his size. Theologian Karl Barth says, "Laughter is the closest thing to the grace of God." Working with P.J. serves as a constant reminder of the truth of these words, that laughter is, no matter the circumstances, evidence of God's presence in our lives.

I had been working for the Lifesaving Crew for less than a year when P.J. and I worked our first serious call together, a cardiac arrest to which my partner Amanda and I had responded at 2:00 a.m. Dispatch had sent us in response to a patient "not acting right," the exact words the 911 caller had used to describe the patient. Dispatch had no reason to also send a fire unit given the protocol to do so requires evidence of a serious medical emergency, and I had no reason to request fire department backup just to treat a patient with such a vaguely worded chief complaint.

Generally, this kind of call results in a patient refusal, but we respond to them emergency traffic nonetheless. On this occasion, that response was in order. Amanda and I walked into a run-down house, in one of the poorest parts of the city, and were met by an elderly lady so stooped that her dirty blonde hair fell into her eyes. Through a fog of smoke rising from her cigarette, she guided us down a narrow hallway, made even more narrow by the stacks of old newspapers lining one wall and rising almost to the ceiling. The newspaper stacks ran the entire length of the hallway. "My husband just ain't hisself tonight," she muttered as we found our way into the farthest room in the house.

Lying on a dirty bed in a cramped room, also stacked with newspapers along the walls from floor to ceiling as the hallway had been, lay her husband, a long wirey man, with a mat of grey hair and grizzled beard. He was not breathing. I had to crawl into the bed to feel for a carotid pulse. He had none. "Amanda, call for a fire unit and bring the trauma bag," I said.

She ran back the way we had come, and I slipped my hands through my patient's armpits and clasped them across his chest. I was able to drag him back down the hallway, stacks of newspapers rocking as I bumped into them, and stretch him out on the living room floor. His wife scurried in front of me. "Is he going to be alright?"

I began chest compressions and waited until Amanda returned with our trauma bag and was able to begin positive pressure ventilations. Captain Bowling from the fire department had been in his response unit and near the scene. He stuck his head in the door. "What do you need?"

"Monitor," I shouted back. When he returned P.J. and the other firefighters on the first response team followed him in. I continued chest compressions. Amanda bagged the patient.

"P.J., can you drop a tube," I said, knowing that the sooner we intubated our patient the better. P.J. flopped his five foot frame into the floor and stretched his legs behind him, while Amanda passed him the laryngoscope and ET tube. P.J. quickly had the tube in place, but when he tried to remove the stylet used to guide the tube it would not budge.

"What the hell . . . this damn thing's stuck . . ." P.J. began before taking note of the setting. "I'm sorry, miss, I know better than to talk like that," he said looking up at our patient's wife. "I really am sorry." She sat observing, no reaction, her cigarette dangling from her lips.

As he apologized, P.J. was able to force the stylet from the tube and attach the bag and begin ventilations. We had good rise and fall of the chest and breath sounds in both lungs. The tube was well placed.

While P.J. was intubating, the captain attached the monitor. We had asystole, or flat line, which cannot be effectively treated with electricity, so it was time to get to the truck and initiate drug therapy. With so much help on scene, we were quickly loaded. While P.J. continued to bag our patient, I was able to gain IV access and give the first rounds of epinephrine and atropine. Amanda moved from the back to the cab of the truck and began our emergency transport to the hospital. The only thing to do was bag the patient, watch the monitor, and continue with drug therapy. Given all the excitement moments earlier, the trip to the ER was relaxed, so much so that P.J.

asked, "Can you hold me an emesis basin?"

"Sure," I responded, wondering what he was thinking. P.J. was dripping sweat and the front of his shirt was soaked, but he did not look ready to vomit. As I held out the basin, P.J. let a long brown stream of spit drop from his lips.

"I been needin' to spit for about ten minutes. Thought I might have to swaller that dip 'cause I didn't want to spit right there in the house."

His mouth now clear, P.J. began to sing, George Jones: "And if drinking don't kill me/Her memory will. I can't hold out much longer/The way that I feel. With the blood from my body/I could start my own still. And if drinking don't kill me/Her memory will."

As he finished the lyrics, he smiled. "We done all we could do for this feller. Ain't up to us no more. When you've done what you can, the only thing's left is to sing George Jones."

We had done all that we could do. In fact, the "code" had, stylet and all, run rather smoothly, much more so than is often the case. Perhaps with his brown-snuff smile and tortured version of a George Jones song did not give the impression of medical excellence. That impression, however, would be false. P.J. demonstrated the extent of his skill and the size of his heart from the moment he entered the scene.

Three years later, P.J. and I worked another cardiac arrest. This time our patient was an elderly female whose body had suffered badly from multiple battles with cancer. Once again, we found ourselves in route to the hospital, the patient intubated and receiving drug therapy for asystole. As we made our way to the ambulance, I said to one of the firefighters, "We aren't going to have a good outcome on this one." Almost as soon as we were loaded in the truck, however, we got a pulse, a strong carotid pulse. I looked up at P.J., who was again bagging the patient while I administered drugs. "What do you sing now, P.J.?" I smiled.

He thought for a moment and then grinned: "Now, the race is on and here comes pride up the backstretch/Heartaches are going to the inside . . ." Amen brother P.J.

There's a reason P.J. Fleenor is the best paramedic I know. No matter what he has seen or experienced, he has kept his perspective about life; it is a gift and one which must, must, allow us the to laugh. Of all the scriptures that reveal God's desire that his children be joyful, none speaks more clearly than Psalms 32:11. "Be glad in the Lord, and rejoice, O rightous, and shout for joy!" For P.J., a country boy from southwest Virginia, shouting for joy simply means singing a verse or two of George Jones. In his joy, P.J. finds his gifts. In his gifts, he discovers his skills and his perspective on life. That perspective, that awareness of both sides of life, of the bad which causes us to grieve and the good which provides our joy, leaves me with no doubt that P.J. is the paramedic that I want on scene when someone I love needs emergency care.

* * * * *

Before I began to work as a paid EMS professional, I relished the sound of my pager when the Helton Volunteer Ambulance Service was being dispatched. Helton is a very small community in the northwest corner of North Carolina. While North Carolina, like all states, has many volunteer rescue and fire departments that operate ambulances, Helton has the only remaining totally volunteer ambulance service. It began in the 1960s to serve the community, using a converted hearse as an ambulance, operated by a group of what were basically first aid trained volunteers. When I had decided to move to the Helton community in 2005, I had studied to become an EMT-Basic in order to help as a volunteer, but had no aspirations to become further involved in EMS and certainly not to become a paramedic.

In 2008, Helton was approved to operate at the North Carolina EMT-Intermediate level, which basically means providing more than first aid and transport but not offering full, paramedic-level treatments. For that the county relies on a professional EMS service that dispatches from Jefferson, North Carolina, approximately twenty-five minutes from the Helton community for an ambulance running hot. I maintained my affiliation with the Helton service after going to work for the Lifesaving Crew, but my eagerness for a dispatch to come in lessened considerably once I was working anywhere from thirty-six to seventy-two hours a week responding to EMS calls.

I could tell, however, in October 2009, just before noon on a Saturday morning, as my wife and I were about to drive to Wilkes County to buy apples for canning, that I better respond to the dispatch the Helton volunteers received. We were directed to a male patient who had cut his leg with a chainsaw. Although the incident could be minor and the dispatch information had not indicated the extent of the injury, chainsaw accidents can be some of the most serious that EMS responders treat. The blade on a chainsaw doesn't just lacerate tissue; it chews that tissue. It tears at the skin and muscle, even the tendons, ligaments, and bone. Living in a rural community, EMS providers quickly learn that two of the most serious injuries they will treat result from chain saw and four-wheeler accidents. If nothing else, the mechanism of injury told me that this was a call I definitely needed to take.

Often, because Helton relies completely on volunteers whose work schedules, like mine, prevent them from being available, no one is able to respond to calls. The professional service in Jefferson is also dispatched anytime Helton receives a call. And the Lansing Volunteer Fire Department overlaps with and provides service to the Helton community. The fact that Helton volunteers are not always available generally poses no real problem. However, as I checked in route that Saturday morning, I heard several other Helton volunteers on the radio. We would need every one of them. The first volunteer on scene, Denver Caudell, did not take an ambulance. The station was on my way, so I contacted him.

"What are we going to need?" I asked.

"We'll be needin' fluids."

I knew from what he said and the tone of his voice that the injury was serious. I contacted Brenda Brooks, who had also checked in route.

"Meet me at the station. We'll take the truck."

Moments later we were in route to the scene, less than one half mile from the ambulance station. Our patient was about one hundred yards from our closest access. A crowd gathered. Brenda grabbed the trauma bag, while I pulled a bag of normal saline from the warmer. I also took my personal bag as I prefer to work with it whenever possible--it is organized exactly the way I want in order for me to work efficiently.

We hurried across a rain-soaked field to where Larry Ham was lying in the mud, barely conscious, pale as new-fallen snow, mumbling but not saying anything that we could understand. Larry had been giving Tommy Sturgill, one of his neighbors, a hand when the chain saw kicked and cut deep into his left leg and through the femoral artery. Tommy was holding direct pressure. Denver had taken Larry's vitals. His blood pressure was nothing over nothing. He was losing blood fast, despite Tommy's best efforts. Brenda knelt in the mud to help Tommy and to listen as he confessed through his fear that he had been holding the saw when it kicked back toward Larry. She helped keep direct pressure on Larry's wound and encouraged him that he had handled the emergency well.

Right behind us, Randy Porter, a brand new North Carolina paramedic who volunteered with Helton, arrived. We had more volunteers on that call than any I could remember responding to a previous dispatch and more were in route. Randy and I each took an arm and began to look for veins. Larry's blood pressure was so low that finding one was not easy. Randy missed his first stick. I was able to slip an 18-gauge needle into Larry's left AC and attach a line of normal saline. Randy's wife held the bag of normal saline, and I instructed her about how to squeeze it at the top and pressure infuse the fluid. Randy was able to start a second line with his next stick, and yet another volunteer brought more bags of saline from the ambulance. With a second line going, we were able to speed the lifesaving fluid replenishment that would lessen the workload on Larry's heart and reduce the likelihood of his suffering a traumatic cardiac arrest.

Underneath Larry, blood covered the ground. The ground was saturated with water from recent rains, so bright red arterial blood ran out from under his leg forming a crimson pool. A severed femoral artery can cause a patient to "bleed out" quickly, but Larry had been cut too close to the groin for us to apply an effective tourniquet. Direct pressure, if pressing the severed ends of the artery against the bone, can help slow the blood loss, but not stop it. Even a rapid infusion of normal saline offered only a short-term solution. It would ease the stress on Larry's heart, but saline does not have blood's ability to circulate oxygen. In our haste to get IV fluids going, Randy and I had not sent anyone to get an oxygen tank from the ambulance and help Larry's perfusion by providing the primary, life-saving drug--O_2. We were late getting to one of the most basic of treatments!

By the time we had two lines of fluids running, the ambulance from town was still a few minutes away, so we had decisions to make. Low hanging clouds and fog prevented us from calling any of the air transport services that serve Ashe County. None of them would have been able to get a bird through the mountains to our location even though we had a perfect landing zone within shouting distance of where Larry was lying. Our best option for getting Larry to definitive care was not available. We could have loaded him into the Helton ambulance for transport, but Larry was at risk to go into cardiac arrest given the severity of his injury.

He needed to be transported to the hospital in a paramedic unit that would have a more extensive stock of cardiac drugs than our ambulance is able to carry.

We waited for the ambulance that was coming from Jefferson. As that truck arrived, I replaced the near-empty bag of saline that I had first started so that Larry would have a fresh 1000 cc running as he was loaded. Before that truck left with Larry, his blood pressure was 127/68. Such a strong response to the fluid infusion suggested he was more stable than when the Helton volunteers had begun working on him approximately fifteen minutes earlier. His chances of not coding were significantly better than they had been, so the biggest challenge now would be to get him to a surgeon to repair the damage to his leg.

Larry was taken to Ashe Memorial Hospital. There, he received several units of blood. He received treatment from a surgeon to stabilize him for transport to Winston-Salem where he was able to receive definitive care. He was released six days later and within two weeks was getting around using a walker and within a month, a cane. Two months later, he was back to a regular routine. Had he not received the rapid and capable treatment from the Helton Ambulance Service volunteers, he would have died. As I would learn later, however, more people than the EMS volunteers had played a vital role in saving Larry's life.

Despite his distress, Tommy Sturgill had known to provide direct pressure to Larry's wound. Had he not done so effectively, Larry would have died before the Helton volunteers arrived. Unable to leave Larry and go for help, Tommy had shouted. Two fishermen along the nearby Helton Creek had heard his shouts and gone for help. Even as those of us with the ambulance service responded, other members of the Helton community gathered to offer their help. Glen Sullivan, whose mother and father had been the first two members of the Helton Volunteer Ambulance Service when it began during the 1960s, arrived and helped Randy's wife hold the second bag of fluids and continue pressure infusion.

God provided the people who were needed on a day when as many as could respond had a role. On a day when a member of the community needed ALS volunteers, somehow we were all at home ready to respond. Our efforts, as well as those of Larry's neighbors, were successful for one reason: we were functioning as servants of God. Paul teaches in First Corinthians: "Now there are varieties of gifts, but the same Spirit: and there are varieties of service, but the same Lord; and there are varieties of working, but it is the same God who inspires them all in every one. To each is given the manifestation of the Spirit for the common good" (12: 4-7). The story of Larry Ham illustrates Paul's teachings well. Whether a bystander or a trained EMS responder or an ALS provider, everyone on the scene was filled with the gift of the spirit of God and working as His instrument.

Later, I saw Glen Sullivan at the little country store that serves the Helton Creek residents and provides a gathering spot for the community. He voiced his belief that Larry had received so much help because it was God's plan that he not die. I had heard that so many times after my MI that the words sounded ironically familiar. Ironic because just as Daryl, Frank, and Geno, all of whom were CPR trained, had been where I needed them eight years earlier, the day that Larry Ham needed someone with the training that I have gained, I was close at hand. So often that would not have been the case. Much more often than not, all of us who responded would have been out of the community. That Saturday, we were all available. More important, however, the day Larry needed Him, God was at his side.

For weeks after that Saturday morning, I was not able to pay for a cup of coffee or country ham biscuit at the community store. If I reached for my cash, the owner would simply say, "That's on me." My neighbors who gather at the store wanted to relive the events that had come close to claiming one of their community. I hesitated to respond to questions. Someone else was always quick to jump in and narrate what had happened, inevitably adding, "You boys saved Larry's life."

I smiled each time I heard it; I was then and remain now proud of what we were able to do. However, I will be the first to add what I think needs to be the final word about Larry Ham: "God wasn't done with him yet." God put the Helton EMS volunteers and Larry's neighbors in Larry's path to do a little of the work for Him.

Chapter Four

Dr. Ahmed, the cardiologist working the emergency room at Baptist Healthsouth Medical Center in Montgomery, took over my care and initially decided that I was not in condition to be sent directly to the cath lab. He stabilized my condition and then turned over my care to his partner, Dr. Wool, because his long-awaited vacation began the day after I was admitted to the hospital. I have heard from a nurse who worked in the ER the night I was brought in that Dr. Ahmed had performed artfully providing me with the initial treatment that then enabled Dr. Wool to order diagnostic and then angioplasty/stent catheterization. What happened over the next three weeks, however, tested me, my family, and the skills of the "dream team" of doctors who assumed my care.

One of the biggest problems that occurs during CPR with assisted ventilations, even when the person or persons doing it are well trained, is that the process pushes air into the patient's stomach. When the stomach becomes too full of air and distends, patients will vomit. Some of that vomit will enter the lungs. Paramedics will usually intubate as quickly as possible in order to direct oxygen into to the lungs, but also to prevent stomach contents from aspirating into the esophagus and then the lungs during chest compressions. Daryl, Frank, and Geno, however, had to rely on mouth-to-mouth ventilations for an extended period. My stomach did distend as it filled with air, and I did end up with vomitus in my lungs. Nothing they could have done would have prevented this from happening. The result, however, was that after being admitted to the cardiac intensive care unit, I developed pneumonia and a pulmonary staff infection. This complication required that I be attended by a pulmonary specialist, so Dr. Seliski joined Dr.

Wool and Dr. Ahmed, bringing a third gifted healer into my team of physicians.

My MI had been caused by a blockage in the proximal left anterior descending coronary artery, nicknamed the "widow maker" because that artery provides oxygen directly to the heart itself and when it occludes, the result is almost invariably that the patient dies. I had survived the attack, but my body, weakened from the initial trauma of the myocardial infarction that led to my heart stopping, had less resistance to the infections in my lungs than it would have had these problems developed under different circumstances. My doctors worked a balancing act in treating the variety of problems. Their job proved to be something like that of a workman trying to repair a dam. As soon as one leak is plugged, another develops.

Despite their efforts, my condition deteriorated until my kidneys began to fail. When the kidney problems developed, the fourth member of the dream team began to care for me, a renal specialist named Dr. Krathapoli. By the time all this had occurred, Dr. Ahmed had returned from his vacation and, though I was technically Dr. Wool's patient, became involved in the decision-making.

After more than two weeks of "plugging leaks," their treatment options had narrowed. The infections were under control. I'd had three angioplasty/stint procedures so that my cardiac circulation was adequate. However, my kidneys were not functioning. My body was ballooning with retained fluid. When Dr. Krathopoli attempted dialysis, my blood pressure dropped to dangerous levels, and he had to discontinue treatment. The same thing happened each time he tried to pull fluids out of my system. My kidneys, however, continued to not function.

After almost three weeks since my MI, my family had to face the reality of my condition. If Dr. Krathopoli and his team could not complete the dialysis treatment, I was going to die. If my blood pressure would not hold during treatment, I was going to die. He and the rest of my doctors called my family for a meeting at which the situation would be laid out for them. The meeting took place on a Wednesday night, three weeks and a day since I had collapsed. It took place on the night when so many churches have their Bible studies and choir practice. Wednesday night was also the night when the prayer group at Aldersgate United Methodist and many other churches in Montgomery would be meeting.

As my parents and my children met with Dr. Krathopoli, Dr.

Wool, and Dr. Ahmed, they were aware that my prospects were not good. When, however, Dr. Krathapoli told them that he would have to complete a dialysis treatment or I would die, they learned that he placed my chances of surviving at less than five percent. He asked whether I had any kind of advanced directive concerning my medical care. My parents and my older daughter Kimberly took in the information quietly. My younger daughter, Kate, who had just turned sixteen and should have been celebrating her new status as a full-blown teenager, became furious at what she thought was the family's acceptance that I was about to die and nothing could change that fact. She left the room in tears. Dr. Ahmed followed her. He found Kate and listened to her confession.

Kate told Dr. Ahmed that God had taken her mother nine months earlier and that He would not take me now. If anyone understood that parents can die young, it was my daughters. Less than a year had passed since they had watched their mother's frail, cancer-ridden body slip into a coma which lasted a week before she died. While Kimberly may have accepted the reality that I was going to die and prepared herself for what she had every reason to believe would happen, Kate refused to let go of the thin thread of hope that Dr. Krathapoli had offered.

Dr. Ahmed listened as she wept and said through her tears that she had experienced too much loss already. He held her as she expressed her anger that the rest of the family was too ready to accept that I would not survive. She could not understand what she saw as giving up hope, as losing faith.

Then he told her, "I treated your father when he was brought to the emergency room. He fought too hard to live then. I think you are right. I don't think God is going to take him tonight."

Kate returned to the private waiting room that had been made available to my family. After about an hour, Dr. Krathapoli returned and announced that my blood pressure was holding. Later, he told them that the dialysis was working. After several hours, he told them that I had survived the treatment. Throughout the city, Christians were praying for me, and even as they prayed, God was responding, and I became Darby's "one in 10,000 man."

Dr. Krathapoli had gambled with my life on Wednesday night. On Thursday morning my kidneys began to function on their own. Late that night I woke up and learned what had happened from Kimberly. I had been in a coma for three weeks and two days. I had slept through the hell that my family had experienced, but woke up in time to celebrate my life, to learn of the great courage of my children, and to discover that God had placed in my path an army of good people and a "dream team" of doctors.

* * * * *

I am a Christian. I believe that the Bible teaches the true God and the nature of His power and His love. However, the four doctors who were God's instruments in giving me back my life belonged to four different faiths. Dr. Wool was a Jew. Dr. Krathapoli, a Hindu. Dr. Siliski, an Eastern Orthodox Christian. Dr. Ahmed, a Muslim. In his conversation with Kate, however, Dr. Ahmed revealed something that my doctors shared, other than being gifted men of science, healers with special skills. All were men of faith. They all believed in a deity whose power is greater than the power of men. Dr. Ahmed told Kate that what was going to happen to me was going to be according to God's plan, not his skills as a doctor, not the skills of the other doctors treating me, but God's will. He told her that his faith led him to believe that God was not ready for me to die.

I may not believe that Dr. Ahmed's religion offers the theology that gives us the full and correct understanding of God, but I do believe despite the fact that Dr. Ahmed serves the true God by knowing that his earthly skills are guided by a power far beyond his own. The night that I survived an imperative treatment, but one also likely to kill me, he demonstrated that the person who trusts in God is also the person who has the ability to love and through that love to bring comfort to those who are struggling to hold onto their own faith. By acting as a man of faith and loving my child, he did even more for me than he did as a physician. He helped her face her life with hope, until I could take back that responsibility myself. He accepted that role, not out of obligation as my doctor, but out of devotion to morality that can only come from being a person of faith. Only by being a man of faith, not just science, would have allowed him to tell Kate that she was justified in her clinging to her own faith that her father would beat the odds.

* * * * *

Dr. Ahmed encouraged my daughter to hold onto her faith that I would live. He validated her conviction to look through eyes that saw "life," not death, as the focus that gave essence to her beliefs, and the framework for life that allowed her to hope. While the faith he encouraged her not to give up was not a religious faith, he gave authority to her desire to cling to a view of life such as provides the foundation for religious belief—a view that accepts the possibility of the improbable—in this case the improbability that I would survive the night, that life would overcome death despite the odds against that happening.

As a cardiologist, Dr. Ahmed would have acknowledged the constant presence of death, just as EMS providers feel it each time they clock in for a shift. I do not think that we are more aware of death than any other person, but since our job is, in a sense, to battle death, we do experience death intimately and readily acknowledge its inevitability. Even when we gain a momentary victory by providing life-saving care in emergent situations, we know, because we see, sometimes nothing we do will save a life. We arrive to find patients who are alive, but who, despite our treatments, die before we get them to the hospital. We watch them die despite our best efforts. We learn to accept death and our limitations. Still, however, we struggle to accept that death is, in fact, every bit as much a component of God's plan as is life. Some calls make this struggle especially overwhelming.

The most difficult calls a paramedic runs are those involving children. Those dispatches, however, that require us to care for a woman in labor pose particular challenges, both to our skills as ALS providers and to our ability to find God in the situations where His presence is difficult to see. Psalms 34:18 reads, "The Lord is close to the brokenhearted and saves those who are crushed in spirit." Nothing is more crushing than for a mother to lose a child because of a difficult labor. No one needs the love of God or faces a more difficult time accepting that God is a loving God more than does a mother who delivers a still-born baby.

One of the first calls that I ran after being certified as an ALS provider was to treat and transport a patient who, according to dispatch, was a nineteen-year-old, in her twenty-eighth week, in active labor. My partner, Matt, and I arrived to find our patient, a girl who might have weighed ninety pounds, in obvious and severe pain, standing over the sink in her bathroom, her amniotic sack hanging between her legs. Tears streamed down her face and vomit dripped from her mouth.

Normally, on scene we take a baseline set of vitals; I wanted to get her immediately to the truck. Fortunately, as quickly as I assessed the situation, Matt and a crew of firefighters came through the door with our cot. One of the firefighters was my friend and former teacher, Mark, whose presence helped me relax. As he approached the back of the house where I was holding my patient steady, I caught his gaze.

"You care to ride in with me?"

"Sure," Mark said, and we went to work, his presence and his calm reshaping the atmosphere in which we treated our patient.

Almost as soon as we loaded our patient, her amniotic sack broke and she soaked the cot. She did not, however, appear to be crowning, although her contractions were strong enough and spaced closely enough together I felt confident that she would deliver sooner, not later. Mark and I would have been stretched to care for mother and child were we to deliver a full-term baby. The thought that we would deliver and provide care for one so many weeks premature terrified me.

In the truck, Mark and I assessed our patient's vital signs, placed her on high-flow oxygen, and hooked her to the cardiac monitor to check her EKG. She was in a sinus tachycardic rhythm, which was, under the circumstances, normal. As I looked for a vein to start her on IV fluids, I knew that she would need a large-gauge catheter if the labor and delivery nurses and her obstetrician were going to be able to use the IV access I gained.

I started an 18-gauge IV and began fluids. Mark checked her a second time for crowning. Matt drove hot to the hospital. We by-passed the ER and took our patient directly to the hospital's Women's Center. Within two or three minutes of our arrival, she delivered a baby that weighed less than a pound and which did not survive long enough for a specialty transport unit to take it to the Johnson City Medical Center Neonatal Unit. This proved to be my first, but by no means last, experience transporting a patient in premature labor.

Approximately a year later, on one weekend shift I responded to two similar calls. On Saturday evening, Dispatch called for my partner, Roy, and me to respond to a patient, "in her twenty-fifth week, in the floor, in severe pain." Dispatch kept the patient on the phone and advised us in route that her doors were locked and that she would be unable to get up and let us in. Fortunately, a fire unit was available and followed us to the scene. Dispatch also sent a police officer. We all arrived at approximately the same time. Observing neighbors quickly contacted the apartment complex manager and told him he needed to come to the apartment and give us entry. We were not able to hear our patient when we called from outside the windows. The decision was obvious; should we break through a door or window. Fortunately, the manager arrived to give us access as we debated that action.

We found her in the floor, a large woman, pale, sweating profusely, in pain so severe that she screamed as we moved her to the stretcher and loaded her in the truck. Roy and I went to work in the back as a firefighter drove us hot to the hospital. As soon as we were able to get basic vitals, I knew our patient was at high risk. Her blood pressure was 82/48. If she coded, we would lose her and the baby.

Roy provided her with high-flow oxygen and monitored her EKG. I tried three times in route to gain IV access without success. Her blood pressure was so low that her veins were simply lying flat. It was, however, so dangerously low that a fluid bolus was vital, yet every vein I tried to access evaded me. The only treatment we could really provide was oxygen, rapid transport, and as detailed a report about our patient's condition as we could relay to the hospital.

The labor and delivery nurses were awaiting us, and as soon as they saw the patient, they assembled a surgical team to perform an emergency C-section.

Later that night, after making another run to the hospital, I learned that our patient had suffered a ruptured uterus, that she had been warned after her previous pregnancy that she should not get pregnant again. She had so desperately wanted another child she had ignored that warning and almost died during the delivery. She had so much wanted a child that she had been willing to risk her own safety to bring a new life into the world. She took a gamble and almost lost her life as a result.

The call was difficult to run; I have rarely felt so helpless in my efforts to help a patient. The very next day, I transported a patient whose placenta had ruptured. Her child died as well. Twice in a weekend I saw that particular kind of despair that results from a mother's loss of her newly born child.

All the weeks of anticipation of a new life ended for each of these mothers with the death of their babies. I found the thought devastating as I remembered the birth of my daughter Kate, as I recalled the joy of cutting the umbilical cord and, in that small symbolic way, participating in her arrival into the world a healthy child. The Seventeenth-Century British poet Ben Jonson, in his short work entitled, "On My First Sonne," laments the fact that as a Christian he could not celebrate the fact that his child died young and traded the pain of an earthly life for the eternal joy of Heaven. As Christians, we, too sometimes feel as Jonson felt, that our faith is not as strong as the message of our beliefs. In the Beatitudes, Jesus speaks of those whose faith is true, "Blessed are you that weep now, for you shall laugh" (Luke 6:21). For a mother suffering the pain of loss, such words are particularly difficult to embrace. Yet, this is the message of Christianity, that the experience that challenges us most to love God and know His presence is the experience that ultimately can bring us closest to God and to know the joy He has promised those whose faith is true.

My experiences in EMS have challenged me to hold my faith as I have witnessed so much pain, so much grief. Yet years before my becoming a paramedic, God prepared me to embrace this message of faith by giving me so many models from whom to learn and by humbling me in the process.

* * * * *

Working the mountains of North Carolina and Southwest Virginia means running a lot of calls to locations lost in the back hollows along winding roads. For my first regular partner Jerry Wiedner, those winding roads once proved his undoing and led to a story that has become infamous within the region's EMS community.

Jerry and his partners Josh and Brandon had responded to a basic sick call from a middle-aged lady who lived in a secluded section of Southwest Virginia. They loaded their patient. Josh drove, while Jerry and Brandon rode with the patient during transport to Smith County Hospital. The ambulance they had taken to the scene was a large box, a style that allowed Jerry and Brandon to sit on either side of the patient. They had established IV access and begun giving the patient normal saline. The effect of those winding roads was, nonetheless, predictable for a patient who called 911 complaining of being "sick" and "needing a ride to the hospital." Her face grew pale, the beads of sweat popped out on her forehead, and her dilated pupils just in time to grab a red bio-hazard bag and thrust its open end in front of her mouth. What we call projectile vomiting followed. Fortunately, Brandon had been able to get the wide-opened bag in place in time to catch the flow. The odor, however, filled the box. The roads continued to wind, Josh maintained his course, Brandon caught the vomit, and

Jerry turned green.

Jerry had lived in the country all his life. He had served in the navy for twenty years, most of it at sea. The odor that engulfed him, however, was too much. At first, he managed to clinch his teeth and hold back the spasms that were rolling over him. His clenched teeth told of his determination to maintain his professional image. Their patient continued to vomit. Jerry grew more and more pale. Sweat dripped from his exertion. His gags became increasingly pained. Finally, with one despite lung, he grabbed the bag from Bandon and added his contribution to its growing contents. He and the patient continued to share the vomit bag to the hospital. Brandon sat back and observed, determined, as he puts it, "to not laugh" at a man who has mentored us all.

At the hospital, Jerry tied up the bag and placed it on the cot to take into the ER to throw away. As he, Josh, and Brandon placed their patient in a room, Jerry picked up the bag and headed for a bio-hazard container. An ER nurse stopped him. "She vomited that much?"

Jerry stopped. Brandon and Josh were unable to control their laughter. The ER staff froze, watching the scene as it developed. They all knew and liked Jerry.

"No," Jerry muttered, "My supper's also in that bag."

God does have a sense of humor. If we are lucky, we realize that being able to laugh when we can is essential, because so often life gives us little chance to grasp the joy that God intends for us. Part of what makes this story reveal the side of God that wants us to laugh is that Jerry could as easily laugh at himself as he could at anyone else who had suffered the same embarrassing experience.

Chapter Five

In January 2001, I was losing control of my life. Not in ways that anyone other than I would know. I knew, however, that I was walking on the edge and that if I fell, my daughters would fall with me.

My first wife, Claire, had died of cancer in August 2000. We had been divorced two years. I felt a profound sense of sadness at her passing, mostly because she never had the chance to regroup from our divorce and enjoy a new life. I felt guilt that I was going to have the chance that she was denied. Even more overwhelming, I found myself with two daughters who needed a strength from me that I was sure I did not possess. Kimberly had begun her life as a single mother with two daughters. She was an adult when her mother passed, but was a very young twenty-five. Her mother had been for her a source of inspiration and a foundation. Kate, at fifteen, was at an age where the loss of her mother would be even more profound. She would not have a model for her teenage years, not the model she needed, not a mother to share the joy and sadness that would accompany her growth into womanhood. Both girls had me. We had strong relationships. However, being the father they needed created demands that I was not prepared to face.

I made sure that Kate ate breakfast before school, that I packed her a proper lunch, that at least two nights a week we ate an evening meal together. I learned to cook the meals she liked. I stressed, probably over stressed given her work ethic, the need for her to keep her grades up. I tried to be available to Kimberly when she was looking for me. I accepted the compliments from people who saw me at PTA and other school functions for being an inspiring single father. I did so with guilt because of the truth that lay behind the façade.

By January I had fallen into a daily routine of teaching my classes, taking care of the business of being a father, then drinking and smoking myself through the night. Sometimes, when Kate was at a drama or choir rehearsal, those nights began early. When she went to a sleep over, those nights began early and ended early, the next morning. I spent long hours on a stool at the neighborhood bar. I talked about nothing with the other regulars, played pool with my friends Dwayne and Stan, and developed a passion for tequila shots. I did not hide my new life from Kate nearly as well as I thought. I did not hide it from myself at all. I did, however, find many excuses to justify the destructive direction my life was going. Then, on a brisk afternoon as I drove by Kate's school, I turned into the parking lot at Aldersgate United Methodist Church. I walked into the church office and met the pastor, Larry Byars.

I told Larry that despite my having been raised in the church, I had not attended services since graduating from college. I told him that in graduate school I had committed myself to an intellectual life, which I could not reconcile with a life of faith.

Larry sat quietly in his office, his elbows on the arms of his chair and his chin resting on the base of his interwoven fingers. He listened as I talked on about the death of my former wife, my efforts to be a suitable father for my children, my steady slide into an increasingly empty life. When I stopped, Larry asked me if we could pray. I nodded, and Larry prayed with me. I was more an audience for his prayer than a partner. When he invited me to attend services, however, I decided that the compulsion that had brought me to Larry's office would not be satisfied unless I accepted his invitation.

The following Sunday, I attended the evening service held in the church's chapel as the thought of entering the sanctuary of that enormous congregation gave me pause. At that evening service, I met the associate pastor, Jason Adams. The moment I met Jason, I knew what had been pulling me to Aldersgate.

Larry Byars had welcomed me back to the Church. Jason Adams welcomed me back to a life of faith. Jason was not a theologian. Had his approach been intellectually aggressive, he would have triggered in me an academic response. I am sure that we might have had some stimulating discussions. Such discussions, however, would have been feeding the part of my life that was already well nourished, not the part that was starved. What drew me to return to the Church was not a need to think; it was a need to believe, to believe in myself, to fill the spiritual void that was pulling me into an empty life. Until I became the remaining parent on whom my daughters had to rely, such an emptiness did not really matter to me. By the time I met Jason, however, I knew that I had to heal. His relaxed and loving approach to his ministry began that process.

Jason's life was a witness to God's power and His love. He had a beautiful family. He and his wife had been blessed with two daughters. Just watching the four of them interact was a testament to the vital life Jason was living. His sermons were Biblically sound, but his manner of showing how Biblical principles served as the basis of everyday life helped me understand how my spiritual emptiness had developed because I had always allowed my academic mindset to guide me. My success in the academic world stood in contrast to my failure outside the walls of the academy. My soul was empty because I had tried to fill it with the same material that filled my mind. It wasn't working. It never had worked. Jason did not reveal to me the answer of a great mystery; he simply preached a message that made clear what should have been obvious. He lived a life that provided an example I could follow, if I wished. And he was not alone.

Within a few weeks of attending evening services, I had met a few other members who, like me, found Jason's style appealing. Each week, his message that God is present in our lives, that all we have to do is learn to see His presence, kept me looking for God and open to the sign that would finally let me grasp the message that my life mattered. All the while, that sign was right in front of me, in Jason and the other members of Aldersgate whose smiles and handshakes, whose honest interest in me, were not just a welcome to Aldersgate, but God's welcome back to His community. They were the revelation I was seeking. Their love was a reflection of God's divine love.

I may not have been understanding this fundamental truth, but I was feeling it. Feeling it brought me back each week, until finally one evening I asked Jason if I could join Aldersgate. He did not suggest that we talk or that I wait until regular Sunday morning services; I joined the church that night. After the service, I was talking with my new friends, the Ellises. In that conversation, I mentioned that I used to play softball. They insisted that I speak with their son, who played for the church's team, which was about to begin practice.

Two weeks later, I was on the practice field getting to know my new team. Again, I found, if I struggled to see God in my own life, I readily recognized His love in the community of men who embraced me with friendship and who, a few weeks later, would save my life with their determination. I found in God's community a place where I was told I belonged, and in my teammates a genuineness that let me believe it. My relationship with the players from my previous softball team had been similar, but with the team at Aldersgate I found that what we did was designed to glorify God, and not ourselves, even in something as simple as playing a game.

When I joined the EMS community after retiring from teaching, I found such a home again. The police, fire, and EMS responders are a diverse group, not connected by a particular faith, but the bond that unites them is fierce and can only be a reflection of the kind of love that Jesus taught when he said, "Greater love has no man than this, that a man lay down his life for his friends" (John 15: 13).

* * * * *

Earl Morphew was killed in January 2009 in a head-on collision when a drunk driver was speeding in the opposite lane of traffic on Interstate 81 just north of Bristol, Virginia. The MedFlight crew dispatched to the scene was the same crew that Earl was in route to relieve. By the time they arrived, the Medic from the ambulance on scene had found Earl dead, and his colleagues at MedFlight treated the driver who had killed him. They could not allow their love for Earl to affect the care they provided, but in the days that followed the fire, police, and EMS community expressed that love in a way that I would never have been able to grasp had I not experienced the same kind of love at Aldersgate United Methodist Church--the kind that reveals God's presence in the world, especially a grieving world.

From the moment I met Earl, I knew that I had found a mentor. I was a student in the Southwest Virginia Paramedic Program, riding a clinical with the Lifesaving Crew, more than a year before I would become a member of that EMS organization. Earl was working with Jay Gouge, one of those people who sees little gray area in life. Earl, however, with his shaved head, granite-firm jaw, and intense dark eyes initially struck me as much more intimidating. I walked into the station to meet them, a fifty-three-year-old man with white hair and beard, wearing a student shirt that belonged on a twenty-year-old kid.

Earl stared through me. "So how'd you end up here, in EMS?" He hadn't even given me his name.

"Well," I stumbled, "I retired from teaching and then went back and taught two years at Emory & Henry College . . ."

"You ever teach a girl named Mallory?"

"Mallory Morphew? One of the best students I have taught in thirty years, if that's who you mean."

"My name's Earl," he said, "Earl Morphew."

Earl loved his daughter with a fierceness that made my one statement bind us into a friendship that enriched my life. Earl expressed his devotion to that friendship by being the most demanding preceptor I ever had as a student, and then an equally demanding partner when I joined the Lifesaving Crew--a job I applied for because he told me I should.

One day I was relaxing in the bunk room during a quiet shift. Earl walked past.

"Jerry, tell me the Parkland formula."

"It's a formula for calculating how much fluid to give a burn patient."

"I know what it's for. I asked you what it is." Never a smile.

"I'd have to look it up the be exact, Earl. I know that you give half the fluid in the first eight hours after the burn and the other half over the next sixteen."

"You got to know it without looking it up," Earl said. Still no smile. "You got to know this stuff."
I nodded.

About thirty minutes later, Earl came back to the bunk room.

"Jerry, you got a 180 pound patient who has second- and third-degree burns over both legs and his abdomen and torso, how much fluid you going to give him?"

I put down my pleasure reading and pulled out my field guide.

"Got to look it up, don't you," Earl said. "I told you, you got to know this stuff. Gave you half an hour to learn it and you still don't know it." Earl walked away, and I went to work getting ready for when he returned in thirty minutes.

The Parkland burn formula is 4 x Patient Weight in Kg x Percentage of Body Surface Area Burned. I learned it before Earl's next visit, and the day he died I said it to myself as a prayer for an amazing paramedic. Mine was perhaps the most peculiar prayer said for Earl that day; it was by no means the only prayer lifted to heaven.

After watching the funerals for the first responders and firefighters who died on 9/11, Earl bought a set of bagpipes and began teaching himself how to play. In addition to being a paramedic, Earl served as both a professional and volunteer firefighter. He would bring his pipes with him to work and during quiet moments would practice in the bays between the trucks. He played at first in a manner that reminded his fellow firefighters that ancient bagpipes had bags made from the bladders animals. Based on their reports, the sounds Earl made with his pipes were not unlike those made by a pig being slaughtered. He applied himself to the task, however, with the same dedication he applied to learning to be a firefighter and to being a paramedic. He became a capable piper, bought himself a kilt and the other attire he needed to dress out as one, and then made himself available to play at funerals for any emergency services responder or family of those responders who wanted him to play. For Earl's funeral, pipers from around Virginia asked to play, and they celebrated with joyful notes the life of Earl Morphew, along with his friends, family, and co-workers from Southwest Virginia.

Earl's viewing and funeral brought emergency response personnel from throughout the region. His casket was carried from the Chilhowie Methodist Church, which his family attended, to the cemetery mounted on a fire truck. The procession passed between two seemingly endless rows of police, troopers, firefighters, and EMS responders. The sun shown the day Earl was buried, but a harsh winter wind burned the tear-stained cheeks of Earl's friends and co-workers. We stood in that wind to offer our part of a tribute to a man who made the world better for having been a part of it. We stood in that cold wind because we loved Earl. He earned our love by being devoted to his calling and to those who shared it.

About a year before Earl was killed, he had finally made it onto a MedFlight chopper as a flight medic. He loved flying and the challenges of treating the patients most in need of a gifted paramedic. Earl was thrilled that he earned his wings as a medic. He deserved those wings, and the gift of having that one year of flying. That year of soaring only prepared Earl for the day his soul would take flight.

I do not know Earl's religious beliefs, nor those of most of the men and women from the world of emergency responders who mourned his passing. I do know, however, that the kind of love that Earl expressed in the manner he lived his life, moving nimbly from stern stare to broad smile, could only exist in a world where God is present. I know that the kind of love expressed by those who cried at his passing reflected, as well, the kind of love that God offers all his children, whether we can, at any particular point in our lives, see it or not. The manner in which we lost Earl challenges us greatly to see God in our lives; the manner in which we celebrated his life after his passing even more greatly affirms that He is there.

Chapter Six

My first reaction to discovering that I had survived a major heart attack was relief. When I learned how my family and I had been so well cared for by my friends, especially those at my church, I felt profound gratitude. As I realized how little had been my odds of survival and how extraordinary the kindness extended to my family, I found myself struggling to accept that I had received such blessings. Those initial life-affirming reactions did not last. Anger quickly followed.

I awakened on a Thursday night. On Friday afternoon, a wheelchair ambulette arrived to take me to a rehabilitation facility. I was still struggling to grasp what lay ahead as I was wheeled from my room, but certainly knew enough to understand that I wanted to go home but was not being released to do so. That anger grew as I arrived at the facility, was moved to my room, and found myself in a bed with an alarm that would not let me move without the nursing station receiving a message and a loud buzzer near my ear shouting its reprimand.

I wanted to go home. I wanted to go immediately. But no one from my family had arrived to make the arrangements. After about an hour, a pretty girl named Heather entered my room, introduced herself and said that she would be directing my therapy. She had flowing blonde hair and bright blue eyes. Despite her scrubs, I was aware of her shapely figure. Heather was young and pretty enough that I was confident that with a bit of persuasion, intimidation if necessary, I could convince her my best interest would be served by my going home.

"All I really need is to go home," I said with confidence.

Heather looked up from the chart she was reviewing. She directed those blue eyes in my direction. "When you're ready."

Silence filled the room.

"Okay, how long do I have to be here?" I asked.

"We're probably looking at five or six weeks."

"No," I responded, "I will be out of here in a week."

"That is not very realistic," Heather smiled, shaking her head. "I'll be deciding when you're ready as we work on your rehabilitation."

"What do I have to do for you to sign off on my leaving?"

Heather explained that I would have to demonstrate certain levels of cognitive and physical capacity to prove that I would be able to care for myself. After that, she recommended that I enter a cardiac rehabilitation program as an out-patient.

After she left, I tried to stay awake. She had her plans for me. As my eyes began to close and sleep captured my thoughts, I was planning my own agenda for the next few days. I struggled to stay awake. My Kate had been through enough, had lived in a disrupted home as long as I was willing to accept. I was going home to her, and was going to do it quickly. I could easily pass the mental capacity tests. As weak as I had grown, I felt equally confident about mastering those tasks requiring physical exertion. I would do both quickly. I would perform the tasks Dr. Wool sent me to the rehabilitation facility to demonstrate.

God, however, had sent me there for a different reason. He was not going to let me return to my family and friends without learning a lesson that had nothing to do with my mental or physical recovery.

God realized that I was not emotionally or spiritually ready for the life ahead of me. My anger was the evidence. That anger was going to receive much more attention at the rehabilitation center than was my mental or physical preparedness. How does God teach us to put aside our anger? With love. And God sent his servants to love me back to emotional and spiritual health.

My arriving at the rehabilitation center on Friday appeared as just another piece of very bad luck, which only fueled my anger. I had been in the hospital for almost a month. During that time, I had lost over forty pounds, almost 20 percent of my body weight. My muscles had atrophied. My beard, normally well-trimmed, had grown along my neck and face. I felt shaggy and dirty. As soon as I was awake on Saturday morning, I asked about shaving, brushing my teeth, and showering. The nurse on duty told me that because of the of the multiple blood-thinner medications Dr. Wool had prescribed, I would be unable to shave, or even have someone shave for me. She added that I would only be able to brush my teeth with the little sponge tooth brushes such as are used with ventilated patients in ICU. I asked to at least be allowed to shower. She told me that I would be allowed to shower while sitting in a chair, but only if attended by a staff member. She pointed out that on weekends, staff were not available to help me and that I would have to wait until Monday.

My anger exploded. All my feelings of relief and thankfulness of just two days before retreated when challenged by my rage. I spent the day complaining about the situation—about my not being able to feel clean, about the fact that I could not move in my bed without setting off an alarm that interrupted any nap I might try to take, about the food that left me wanting only one thing—a chocolate milkshake—which I could not get. My parents had left on Friday. They returned to their home to back in North Carolina to attend to their affairs, long neglected at this point. Their plan, unless something changed, was to return in a week. With me out of danger at the hospital, both my daughters visited me at the rehab hospital but were working their jobs to make up for so much lost time during the three previous weeks. I understood what each of them had to do and did not feel abandoned. I did, however, feel trapped. And I was furious.

At approximately 6:00 p.m. on Saturday, Louis, an orderly working my hallway, came to my room. He walked through the door and came to my bed and unhooked the alarm.

"Come on, man," he said.

I looked at him, trying to understand.

"Come on. You want a shower, don't you?"

"Yeah, but . . . "

"Then come on."

"Isn't your shift over?"

"Yeah, do you want a shower, or not?"

Louis helped me into the shower chair, turned on the water, and adjusted the temperature. He stood while I soaked and bathed for the first time in almost a month. I let the warm water roll over my body. Louis didn't offer to help me shave. He did, however, on a Saturday night when most young men his age would have been fleeing work in order to enjoy a night-out with their girl friends, stand where he could keep an eye on me and make small talk. When I was finally finished, Louis helped me dry, get into a clean pair of pajamas the girls had left, returned me to my bed, and reattached the alarm.

As Louis stepped toward the door, I stopped him. "Thanks...I--"

"Yeah, take care, man. See you Monday."

I lay back in bed and savored the feeling of being clean, and dosed for about an hour. When I woke up, my colleague from school, Craig Sheldon, was in my room. I was delighted to see him. Though still new to the facility, I did know that visiting hours were over. We chatted a while about what had been happening at the university. Then I paused a minute.

"Is it okay for you to be here?" I finally asked.

"It's okay. I'm going to stay tonight so that they can unhook the alarm on your bed. Seems you've been complaining about not being able to sleep." I smiled. I wanted to visit with Craig but was unable to remain awake long enough to enjoy his presence.

Several times during the night, I woke up. Craig had moved a chair to the corner of the room and was reading under a dim light. When my breakfast was delivered Sunday morning, Craig slipped out. The alarm was reattached, but I felt rested. My anger was not gone, but I was not unaware of the gifts I had received.

Then, around lunch time, a former colleague from the university, Jim Barfoot, whom I had not seen in years, walked into my room carrying a large chocolate milkshake. Craig's coming to help me get a good night's sleep had not been a particular surprise. We had been friends for years. Jim and I, however, had been colleagues but never had more than a professional relationship. I knew the goodness of his heart from watching him work with students. Craig and I were fishing buddies. I had never been around Jim on any occasion other than a work-related gathering. Still, he brought a chocolate milkshake to the rehab hospital every day until I was released. All he said that first day was that he had heard from Craig I had been wanting one.

My rage, a rage enhanced by my not feeling clean or rested or well-fed, was not gone. God had, however, sent messengers who helped me begin a process I needed to complete before going home. He began this process by allowing me to witness the type of kindness that had been extended to my family while I was in a coma. My physical needs had been addressed. My greater needs, the ones which He sent me to the rehabilitation unit to more specifically work on, were yet to be fulfilled, and He was quick to send other messengers to do His will. One lesson that I was quickly learning, however, was that regardless of what we sometimes feel as we face the frustrations of our lives, people are, they truly are, fundamentally good and loving. The love they express is a direct reflection of the divine love of God; we just have to recognize that they are the mirror in which we can see that reflection.

*****

One of the great frustrations of living in a small community, especially a small and isolated community in the mountains, is that everybody knows everybody. That familiarity also generates one of the particular blessings of living in such a location as well. Not long after I became a certified EMT-Basic and moved to the Helton Creek community in Ashe County, North Carolina, however, I saw just how special living in such an intimate community can be.

The moment I heard the dispatch for first responders on a Saturday night, I knew the address. The dispatch was for an elderly female with difficulty breathing.

"That's Aunt Rose," I said to JeDonne as I scrambled to the door.

Aunt Rose lived with my cousin, Russell, only a mile from our cabin, so I was the first emergency responder on scene. Russell met me at the door and led me down a small hallway where Aunt Rose was lying in the floor, unresponsive. We placed her on an oxygen mask, and I began to check her vital signs. Almost as quickly as I was able to kneel in the floor next to her, she quit breathing. The pulse I had initially found was gone. I began CPR. With the first compression I felt the ribs on her frail body crack. Even knowing that ribs often break during CPR, and that sometimes the best way to push the heart against the spine when compressing the chest was to break the ribs, the sound sickened me. She was not just a patient. She was my aunt. She had treated me as one of her own when I was growing up. My cousin was hovering in the hallway watching. Sweat dripped from my face and rolled down my arms. My arms ached as we tried to will Aunt Rose back to life. Suddenly, the house was full.

Aunt Rose had taught French at Ashe County High School for almost forty years. She was, for most of that time, the only foreign-language teacher in the county. Essentially every student in the county who did not drop out of school eventually ended up taking her class. Even county residents who had not done so knew her. As is so often the case in small, rural communities, much of the social life for both students and adults revolves around the high school activities--ball games, fund raisers, theater and choir performances. Aunt Rose had involved herself with most of those activities as a sponsor or booster. She had equally committed herself to the Helton United Methodist Church. If someone in Ashe County did not know her, that person surely knew of her.

By giving Aunt Rose's address, Dispatch might as well have been giving her name. Everyone knew where she lived. Although I had been close enough to be the first responder on scene, I had not been performing CPR long before noticing that Aunt Rose's house had suddenly filled with firemen and first responders. All over our part of the county, emergency responders had probably said the same thing that I said to JeDonne, something like, "That's Rose Kirby. I have to go!"

Just as quickly as I had jumped from the sofa in my cabin, they would have left their homes on a cold night in case they could help. So quickly did Aunt Rose's house fill that we were almost tripping over each other to continue CPR until an ambulance arrived. Even the ambulance crew was comprised of two EMS responders who had taken classes with Aunt Rose and brought their personal involvement to their professional response.

The paramedics were able to restore a heart rhythm by giving Aunt Rose epinephrine and atropine. What became obvious at the hospital, however, was that her cardiac response was entirely drug induced and that she would not survive. She died three hours later, and Ashe County lost a much-loved member of the community.

Watching the emergency responders react to the dispatch to Aunt Rose's house was much like watching the people who came to the rehabilitation hospital to help me, like seeing Jim Barfoot walk into my room carrying a chocolate milkshake. That crowd of mountain community volunteers was not going to be able to make a difference in Aunt Rose's outcome. They were, however, able to stand side to side with my cousin Russell as he made the decisions he needed to make. They were able to help him contact his brother and sister. They were able to share his loss as he began to mourn the passing of his mother.

If I have enjoyed no other experience since becoming an EMS responder, the opportunity to see community volunteers offer themselves to their neighbors has reinforced what I learned during my own health crisis--that the people of God really are servants to His will and to each other. Watching, as well as working with, EMS volunteers, however, has shown me more than just their eagerness to assist their neighbors; they respond just as quickly to assist anyone in need. In The Gospel According to Matthew, Jesus explains to his disciples how their actions to nurture anyone in need are the same as if they had nurtured the Lord himself: "Truly, I say to you, as you did to one of the least of these my brethren, you did it to me" (25: 40). Watching volunteers respond in their communities, I can see the message in this passage manifest. I see it in my own efforts as a volunteer as well as in my professional role when responding to assist volunteer crews in the county.

* * * * *

I had not even finished my paperwork on a call or left the hospital on a cold, Tuesday night in February when Dispatch called the ER radio room to find me and my partner, Michael. We were dispatched to the county to provide ALS assistance at the scene of an "overturned vehicle." Because we happened to be at the hospital, we were, luckily, within a few miles of the accident. As we left the hospital, we heard Crew members, who were at the building for training, check in route to bring our heavy rescue truck to the scene. While having that truck on scene might end up being overkill, with an overturned vehicle any scenario was possible. "Better to have it and not need it than to need it and not have it!" How often had this lesson been drilled into my head, at every level of my EMS education!

When we arrived on scene, the county crew had an ambulance ready, a fire engine illuminating the scene with its side lights, and half a dozen volunteers crawling over a van, lying on its side in a ditch. One was dangling from the passenger-side window, his legs in the air, but the rest of his body positioned in the vehicle so that he could assess the patient's condition. Another had broken through the back windows and gained access to the patient. He was also in a position to see exactly what would be required to extricate the patient and provide him care during the process. The rest of the county crew were making sure the vehicle was stable and the equipment they needed at hand.

Michael and I were on scene in a medical-support capacity. However, we both had extrication training, enough at least for me to know that the position of the vehicle and the location of the patient inside posed some problems. I stepped through the broken-out back window to get a clearer picture and to ask the volunteer inside what he thought would be the extrication time. I found myself standing in a ditch where the side windows had been smashed. My mud-covered boots began to fill with water.

The volunteers had been able to place an oxygen mask on the patient. He was, however, bundled between his seat and the dash. His legs were entrapped by the passenger seat.

"How'd he end up like that?" I asked.

The volunteer, whose name I never got, responded, "He's just sorta wedged in there. Doesn't seem to mind too much."

"How long to get him out?"

"We're gonna unbolt that seat and get it out. See if we can get his legs free."

"But you can't tell how long?" As we talked, I could feel the cold water in the ditch begin to fill my boots.

"Not really."

I checked my patient quickly, determined that he was minimally responsive and breathing then moved back out of the way of the extrication crew.

"Okay, shout at me if he seems to start having trouble breathing," I said as I moved toward the broken back window and onto the side of the road to organize our medical response once the extrication had been completed.

While I was in the van, the Crew's heavy rescue truck arrived. We really didn't need the equipment, so I asked the crew members on it to see about getting MedFlight and setting up a landing zone. I touched base with the trooper on scene and tried to see how the work was going unbolting that seat from the bottom of the vehicle.

After a couple of minutes, the volunteer hanging through the passenger-side window shouted that the patient was beginning to "guppy"—a term used to refer to a breathing pattern that manifests as pursed lips and shallow, gulping breaths. I moved back inside the van and this time reversed positions with the member of the county crew who was working on the extrication. We did not have the luxury of extricating the driver before providing supportive medical treatment.

My patient had knocked the tubing from the oxygen tank to the mask loose and was struggling to breath. I was able to reconnect the line. However, finding his skin cold and no palpable radial pulse, I knew we were going to have to work as fast as we could with the extrication but continue to treat during the process. Doug, one of the Crew members who had been checking about getting a chopper, crawled in the back and told me that the weather was keeping MedFlight on the ground. Michael also had his head stuck in the back window.

"Michael, get me a starter kit, a couple of 18-gauges, and spike a bag of ringers" (lactated ringers is the preferred fluid for trauma patients). I would have preferred using larger-gauge needles, but was going to have a difficult time getting to my patient's right arm. He had an open fracture to the left arm, so I really had only his right arm for starting an IV. I did not want to risk blowing the one or two veins I was able to get access to in cramped quarters.

Over the next several minutes, the volunteers continued to unbolt the seat trapping the patient's legs. Michael and Doug passed me the equipment I needed. My patient fought with me as I tried to straighten his right arm and hold it steady. The three of us in the van, as well as the one dangling in the window, managed to hold him still enough that I got one line running wide open. Although I did not know what injuries he had, if I could not feel a pulse in his wrist he must have a dangerously low blood pressure and needed as much fluid as I could infuse into him.

Finally, the seat was unbolted. Inside the van, I held the patient's arm straight with one hand and helped with a crowbar to pry the seat loose. Behind me, the volunteer with whom I had been working and Doug also pulled at the seat until we had it loose. As they dragged the seat out the back, knives, tools, empty beer bottles and open boxes of nails rained down on us!

"Damn!" we chorused as we ducked the rain of sharp objects. We got a long board into the van, grabbed arms, and belts, and sleeves—whatever we could grab—and pulled the patient free. I have no idea how that IV line of fluids remained intact, but it did.

When I crawled out, the volunteers had converged on the patient. He was immobilized and in a c-collar. They were cutting away at his clothes. He had an open fracture just above his left elbow, so I chose to not start an IV below that fracture. As we prepared to load in their ambulance, I got in with some of their crew and my partners to prepare for an emergency transport. Four of us treated in route, such as we could. Running hot on country roads makes treatment difficult, but we were able to deal with the basics: airway, breathing, circulation.

At the ER a trauma team awaited. Our patient continued minimally responsive. His blood pressure was dangerously low despite my efforts at bolusing fluids. His breathing was compromised and his oxygen level diminished according to the instruments. However, he was cold enough that his reduced skin temperature would interfere with the readings we could gather from a pulse-oximeter.

The next day, I learned the extent of my patient's injuries. He had several fractured ribs as well as the compound fracture to the arm. He had a ruptured spleen, lacerated kidney, and a collapsed lung. He'd had extensive internal bleeding. He had, however, survived surgery and been admitted to intensive care. Without question, given the nature and extent of his injuries, the ability of the volunteers to get to the scene and extricate the patient had saved his life. No one knew him. He was simply a lone driver who had flipped his van—fortunately in a community where the folks volunteer as emergency responders to help their neighbors and those who are simply passing through—including among them the ones who might be deemed "the least" of those.

Chapter Seven

By the time Heather visited my room at the rehab hospital on Monday morning, the kindnesses that had been extended to me had eased my anger, but not my impatience. I was ready to prove I could achieve the goals she had described for me the previous Friday. We began by my meeting the team of therapists who would be working with me. They were all specialists in physical, cognitive, and occupational therapy. Each described what I would need to accomplish and how we would prepare for my release. Heather continued to stress that the objective was for me to be able to care for myself. I continued to insist that I was confident that I could care for myself and needed only to prove that to her. Even as we discussed my therapy, my impatience turned to frustration and my frustration inched back toward anger. I wanted to like Heather, but could only frame her in my mind as my adversary — the one person standing between me and my opportunity to go home. She stood between me and my ability to enable Kate to have her life back, a life that did not obligate her to visit hospital rooms. She'd had enough of that when her mother was sick and did not need one day more of that routine because of me.

After the meeting, Heather took the handles on my wheelchair and directed my path toward my room. I moved my hands to the wheel handles and wrestled control away from her. She said nothing as we continued. As we arrived at the wing of the building where my room was located, I read a sign on the wall that indicated patients in those rooms had suffered brain damage.

"What in the hell is that?"

Heather needed nothing more than my inelegant outburst to know my thoughts.

"Dr. Wool knew your heart had stopped. He wasn't sure how

long your brain might have gone without oxygen, and since you've been--"

"There's nothing wrong with my brain!"

"No, just your attitude! I see plenty of self-pity there."

My head snapped. My jaw dropped as I focused on her eyes.

She did not blink. She did not look away. "OK," Heather said, as a smile crossed her face and we continued back to my room. She left me at the door. "We'll see you after lunch."

I was one day short of four weeks since collapsing. By all accounts I should have died, but God, for what reason I could not grasp, had allowed me to live. Everything that I had learned since waking up should have told me to feel blessed. All I could think about that Monday as I sat in my room was going home. I had begun the morning with a bit of peace about the days ahead. Learning that I was being treated as a brain-damaged patient stole that peace from me. I was not able to see any of my blessings.

I managed to eat and even grab a nap before finally going to work.

My first therapy session was designed to exercise and test my cognitive capacity. The tests demanded nothing more than short-term recall. I sat in front of the computer playing games that tested my ability to remember a sequence of numbers or colors after they had flashed on the screen. By the end of the scheduled hour, I had demonstrated the necessary level of competence to be released from the hospital.

"Guess there's nothing wrong with my brain," I sat thinking, waiting for Heather to take me to my next session.

My next session was, if anything, easier. I worked with an occupational therapist on what seemed to me simple coordination skills. Again, by the time our session ended, I had performed at the level that would allow Heather to release me from her care. I felt torn after the first two sessions. I felt justified by my assertions of being ready to go home, but the more I felt justified, the more I figured my initial anger had been warranted. I was also aware, however, that while none of this was physically demanding, I was tiring quickly.

"You're doing very well," Heather said as she followed me down the hallway. I was still "confined" to a wheel chair, but she had not offered to push since our earlier episode. "Let's go to the gym."

In the gym, I was surrounded by my fellow patients. I had not really noticed any of them previously, even though we had passed in the hallways. I found myself suddenly surrounded by patients who had suffered strokes, serious heart attacks—in some cases for the third or fourth time--, amputations. They were fighting to perform physical tasks that I considered insignificant. Many, however, were struggling. Most wore determined expressions. I focused on a patient whose name, I would learn, was Harold. His eyes were smiling as he worked with simple stretching exercises.

As I watched that room full of straining men and women, as I watched Harold smile because of his ability to do the simplest of tasks, I again felt the sting of Heather's comment about self-pity. Not one person in that room would have the chance that I had in front of me—to return to a healthy, physically complete life. Having wasted a lot of thought on myself, I was ashamed.

I looked up at Heather. "I'm ready when you are."

She nodded, locked the wheels on my chair, and directed me to my first exercise, to a place right next to Harold. Finally, in the gym, I was at home. I knew what to do and began to stretch muscles which had atrophied badly during the past month of inactivity. Next to me, Harold continued his own limited efforts to use a body which age had robbed of its vitality.

Harold looked to be in his seventies or eighties. A thin strand of greasy gray hair hung over his forehead. A stubbled beard covered his thin face. His over-sized ears sprouted thick tufts like weeds which matched the untended crop that grew above his eyes. His lanky body was frail, and his teeth, the few that remained, were yellowed.

He continued his exercises and then spoke. "I'm a-gonna get married onc't I'm done here. She'll give me another heart attack, but I'm a-gonna marry her anyhows."

"Sounds like a plan to me." I caught a glimpse of Heather standing to my side, watching me. Her face was a mask, but behind it I was beginning to think must lie a wealth of compassion. I had surely been assigned the therapist I needed, the one God had sent.

I spent the next two days working in the gym as if preparing for the next season of softball. Every moment that I was allowed, I pressed through the exercises that Heather had prescribed for me. She had freed me from the wheelchair on Tuesday morning. Then on Wednesday afternoon, as I was finishing up my routine for the day, I noticed across the room as one of the therapists was working on a mat with a woman who had just had knee-replacement surgery. At well over three hundred pounds, she struggled to keep her round body from rolling away. Sweat had soaked her short dark hair and was dripping onto the floor. Her therapist tried to get her to bend the knee, I remembered how painful that process had been after my own knee surgery.

I walked over and sat next to her. "I know how bad that hurts," I said. "I've been through these exercises."

Her therapist gave me a look that said to continue. The woman bit her lip and stared through a shower of sweat.

"Once you get that knee back just one time, the rest will come easy," I said.

She struggled through her pain and was able to achieve the ninety-degree angle the therapist was after.

"That's great," I said. "What's your name?"

"Donna."

"You did a good job, Donna." As I stood to return to my own workout, Heather was standing across the room and caught my eye. I walked over and shook my head. "I remember how bad that hurts. She did well."

Heather nodded. And then the slightest smile began to form. "We're releasing you tomorrow. Thought you might want to go back to your room and get ready to go home."

My six weeks had turned into six days. In that short time I had been able to demonstrate what Dr. Wool demanded. More important was that those six days gave me a chance to see something God demanded that I see--just how fortunate I was. To see that, however, I had to first see real suffering, the suffering of those whose bodies would never recover. I had to witness real strength, the strength to accept that we sometimes never recover from our physical losses but do not have to forfeit our spirits as well. Ecclesiastes says, " . . . the race is not to the swift, nor the battle to the strong, nor bread to the wise, nor riches to the intelligent, nor favor to the men of skill: but time and chance happen to them all" (9:11). God demanded that I learn to accept what I could not control and embrace the life he had blessed me with, including my limitations. And in the humility of the elderly and stricken I had begun to see the source of true strength.

I looked at Heather, and tears formed in my eyes. "Thank you."

This time her smile lightened her face. It was a smile of joy. And it illuminated the room with the brilliance of God's love.

Never Alone in the Back
*****

I had not been to apartment 46 ¹/² on a previous call. The numerics seemed odd, but my partner, Bo, and I had driven around in circles for several minutes and then parked the ambulance to look on foot. We found apartments 46 and 47. Both were dark, and no one answered when we knocked. Finally, at the end of the parking lot, near apartment 46, we noticed a light glowing in an outdoor tool shed. "You think?" I asked Bo.

"Guess we can look," he responded. We walked over to the shed and knocked. A rather frail but elegant looking elderly lady answered. She was shaking. She had a stethoscope wrapped around her neck, the ends hanging over her shoulders.

"Did you call 911?" Bo asked.

"Yes."

"May we come in," Bo continued.

She stepped aside and we were able to squeeze into what was perhaps a 12 x 12 foot tool shed set up as an apartment.

"What's the problem, ma'am?" I asked.

"I can't hear my heart. I think it's stopped."

"Excuse me."

She reached for her stethoscope, put in the ear pieces, and then placed the chest piece just above her left breast. "I can't hear my heart. I think it's stopped."

Bo and I spent fifteen or twenty minutes on scene. We learned that our patient was living in the shed because she thought that the people in the apartment above hers were making drugs and that she was in danger. We assured her that her heart was beating, got her to sign a refusal form, and left. For the next three weeks, she called with the same complaint, repeatedly. The police talked with her. They contacted her son and tried to get him involved. Each time she called 911, Dispatch was required to send a medical unit; however, the Crew members made those runs as brief as necessary in order that the ambulance would not be tied up in the event of a real emergent situation.

About three weeks after this string of calls began, I was working with my former teacher, Mark Smith, when I received my second dispatch to apartment 46¹/². Mark had heard about the calls, but not yet met our "frequent flyer."

As we responded to the call, I filled Mark in on my previous experience when Bo and I assured our patient that her heart was in fact beating. "Let's just get a refusal and be done with it," I said as we pulled up.

"That's where she lives?" Mark asked as I indicated the tool shed at the end of the parking lot. Mark's dark eyes were wide and what has been described by one of the paramedics with whom we work, his "Howdy Doody" smile crossed his face.

"That's it. $46^{1/2}$."

Mark led the way as we squeezed into the apartment. Our patient looked more frazzled than usual.

"Hey," Mark smiled, "What's going on today."

"My heart's stopped beating again. It keeps doing that," her voice wavered.

"Well, let me check," Mark said. I stood back, folded my arms, and leaned against the door. He clearly did not understand what I meant when suggesting we get a refusal and leave. Mark listened to her heart sounds, took her blood pressure, and completed an initial medical assessment such as we normally do on scene with medical patients.

"Well, your heart's beating," Mark said.

"Are you sure?"

"Yes ma'am, I hear it. And your blood pressure is good."

"Well, why can't I hear it? I have a stethoscope."

"Let's have a seat," Mark suggested. My eyes rolled back as I realized what was happening. "I think you're just getting scared, but I hear your heart beating. In fact, I was pretty sure that it was beating when you met us at the door,

"How could you tell so quickly."

"How could I tell? Well, you were standing up and talking to me." His voice was as direct and as calm as if he were explaining something that made sense, not talking with a patient who was so obviously not mentally equipped to think or act reasonably.

"You could tell from just that. I use a stethoscope, but I don't hear it." The strain from the almost three weeks of repeated panic episodes was showing. She was shaking as she talked with Mark. Her little shed/apartment was cluttered, even more than on my first visit. Her housecoat looked as if it had not been washed in days. Mark continued sitting at the edge of the bed, his voice focused and calm.

"Well, I could hear it with mine."

"Why do you think that is?"

"It's one of the things we study in paramedic school. You can't hear your heart with yours because it's kind of tricky. You have to learn just how to listen."

"Could I take that class?" I knew we wouldn't be leaving anytime soon when she asked that. The teacher in Mark was just getting started. In fact, we spent forty-five minutes on scene as Mark explained about paramedic classes, how stethoscopes work, why she wasn't able to hear her heart beating, how if she was able to call 911 that was a good indication that her heart was beating. The entire time Mark never talked with her as if she was a child or a disturbed adult. He reasoned with her, but did so in a way that helped her calm down.

Two days later, she again called 911 and told Dispatch that her heart wasn't beating and the duty crew responded.

According to Bible scholars and Christian historians, the disciple Mark hosted the gathering of Jesus' disciples at which the resurrected Christ presented himself and during which the Holy Spirit descended upon the group. With that in mind, I realize how appropriately my teacher, my partner, and my friend Mark is named. He is a tall, lanky man with dark features, a ready smile, and a generous heart. He is a man filled with the Holy Spirit who takes his faith seriously and who lives that faith. His capacity for kindness seems boundless at times. We have run a range of calls, from the absurd to the extremely serious. After one frustrating call, Mark said to me, "If you ever see me not caring, you tell me." That is one conversation that I know will never take place. It is not in Mark's makeup to not care. Spending forty-five minutes watching Mark explain to a lady why her being able to talk indicates that her heart is beating is all the reassurance I need about that matter.

Chapter Eight

The single most obvious connection between my experience as a survivor and as a paramedic has been and remains the effect on my view of life and death, especially how I view suicides. I have learned to cherish life while, perhaps even because of, being aware of the constant presence of death. I have treated patients who have fought to live. I have responded to calls for patients whose age and illnesses have finally left them broken and ready to accept death. I have seen patients live who I initially thought had little chance to survive. I have seen patients die who seemed, initially, in no danger.

For years, as I taught mythology, I discussed with students the natural order of the life cycle and the symbols and rituals in mythology that celebrate it. Nowhere in world belief systems is that natural cycle, and the idea that out of death comes life, realized as it is in Christianity and in the eternal life that Jesus' death and resurrection made possible for all believers.

In the world of EMS, however, the struggle to accept death takes on its most fundamental form, away from the rituals and symbols. In the world of EMS, death is the enemy and sometimes the inevitability. The deaths are difficult to accept, particularly when the patient has committed suicide. Even the death of a child, as horrible as it is, takes its place in the natural cycle. A suicide, however, whatever the cause leading to such despair, denies not only the natural cycle of life, but rejects the willingness of God to love us under all conditions. Ecclesiastes 7:17 asks "why should you die before your time?" I have often found myself asking that question when responding to a call. One occasion, early in my career when I was an EMT-Basic, I found myself feeling a particular sadness to see the effect of a suicide.

Never Alone in the Back

One quiet Sunday afternoon, my partner Jerry and I were called to the scene of a "possible self-inflicted wound." Our dispatch location was within five minutes of the station. Police had arrived just ahead of us and were waving from a downstairs add-on apartment in what had been the basement of a large brick home in an upper middle-class neighborhood. Because the day had been so quiet and the dispatch information so ominous, another crew member, Scott, had brought a second truck. He helped me unload the cot as Jerry made his way through the gathering crowd of neighbors and law-enforcement officers. Scott tossed our trauma bag on the cot and we followed, leaving our equipment just outside the door.

As we walked in, the scene was quiet, much too quiet. Jerry was leaning over a young woman, her face down in the pillows on her bed and a large portion of her head a bloody mass. She was alive. Her father stood behind Jerry, frozen, his eyes empty. Jerry looked up. "Let's use her sheets to carry her to the cot."

Scott and I, with the help of the officers on scene, lifted the sheets with ease. Our patient was long, but frail, so light that any one of us could easily have scooped her into our arms. As we moved her, a small pistol slipped out from under her body and onto the sheet. We placed her on the cot and began to secure the straps. One of the officers reached for the gun. Seeing the pistol, her father slipped to his knees and began to weep, his hands clawing at his shoulders. Even more than the sight of his daughter lying in her blood, the image of this man, broken and alone, has remained with me whenever I have replayed this call in my mind. I would later learn that just the day before, his daughter had asked him if she might have a pistol for protection, and he had provided her with the gun found lying in her sheets.

As quickly as Scott and I secured and loaded our patient, Jerry began to treat and directed me to leave immediately, to run hot to the hospital, and to call with a preliminary report. Usually, the treating paramedic will give the in-route report. With emergent patients, however, the better course is often for the medic to be freed from that duty. Scott joined Jerry in the back to lend his help.

We were so close to the hospital that with running hot, Jerry had little time to treat. Our patient's needs, however, were so pronounced that prehospital protocols would have little effect. Jerry was not able to intubate because of the way her teeth were clenched. To RSI her, to relax and then paralyze her muscles, in order to insert an ET tube would have been risky and inappropriate with such a short transport time. Jerry was able to get basic vital signs, IV access, and an ECG strip printed. The primary treatment for this patient was what emergency responders call a "diesel bolus," jargon for a rapid transport.

Nothing Jerry was able to do or not do for our patient would, or could, change her outcome. Nothing that the ER staff was able to do would matter either. Although her heart continued to beat, she lacked the brain function to live and was placed on life support. Four days later, her family signed the authorization to discontinue treatment, and she died. Ironically, they were forced to finish what she had started when she decided to end her life.

From a distance, without ever approaching her parents or introducing myself as one of the EMS crew who had responded to the call for their daughter, I observed their grief through the newspaper reports and the inevitable chatter of a small community. They suffered a kind of pain that I could not imagine. Perhaps what engaged my reaction to this call, however, was that while I could not imagine what this young woman's family was feeling, I had at least some familiarity with the kind of despair that led their daughter to her decision.

The year before my heart attack, I may have presented one image to the world, an image of strength, of being a capable single parent. What lay behind the image was different. I was systematically drinking and smoking myself to death. I was also living with a combination of stress and sadness that not only fed my reckless behavior but was also creating a mindset of defeat. I struggled to watch my daughters cope with the death of their mother. I questioned why after our divorce I had received a second chance to build a new life, but she had not. She deserved that chance but had been denied even the possibility of being happy again. I looked back over the past several years and saw nothing but mistakes. These thoughts did not visit on occasion; they accompanied me like a faithful dog, ever at my heels, ever in my mind and my heart.

Leaving school one day, I walked through the parking lot outside my office building with my friend Craig (who would in the not too distant future so kindly spend the night with me at the rehab hospital). I finally confessed my guilt. We talked a few more minutes when Craig abruptly asked, "How many guns do you have now?"

"Just the two," I answered, searching his face.

"I think it might be a good idea if I kept them a while."

I looked at him hard, but without speaking, which encouraged Craig to continue.

"Just something in your voice."

I had known Craig for long enough to not argue. I trusted his judgment. Whether I had admitted it to him, or even to myself, my thoughts had taken a dangerous turn over the past few weeks. Although I had not even thought the word "suicide," I had been feeling the need to be relieved from my guilt and sadness, over what had happened to Claire dying so young, over the poor job I felt I was doing for my girls, over hearing words of praise for the life I was living from very generous people who had no idea about the reality behind the image. Being dead meant being free from all those feelings. Most of all it meant being able to rest, finally to rest.

Craig heard enough to make him take my guns that day. In less than a month, I was attending Aldersgate. Craig, however, kept my guns for a year.

For a person suffering emotional distress, whatever its source, suicide may seem, ultimately, the only source of relief. Taking one's life, however, does not end suffering; it transfers it to others. To the father who provided a gun to protect his daughter, only to see her use it to take her life. To parents who must take their daughter off life-support and then live their lives with the inevitable question about whether they made the right decision. Turning to a gun or pills is not the answer to despair. Turning to God is, and He is waiting for us every moment of every day, no matter how tortured those moments and days become. Psalms 42: 5 reads:

Why are you cast down, O my soul,
and why are you disquieted within me?
Hope in God; for I shall again praise Him,
my help and my God.

God is always with us. He never departs. Even when we do not see Him, the darkness is our creation, not God's. He asks only that we turn to Him. My "turning" to God really began the day Craig took my guns from my home. Even if I was not yet to the point of considering ending my life, I was to the point of losing it to my increasingly reckless behavior. Craig's gentle nudge, followed a few weeks later by my visit with Larry Byars at Aldersgate, allowed me to find a path back to God and to discover that in His love we can find a greater relief from the difficulties of the world than can be found in any other decision I might have made.

Sadly, most of the suicides I have seen as a paramedic have been young people. According to the National Mental Health Institute, in 2006, suicide was the third leading cause of death for young people ages fifteen to twenty-four. If only these young people could love themselves as God loves them. If only they could see, as I was blessed to see, through the servants God puts in our path, the love He feels for us. If only they could measure the value of their lives as God measures that value. Christianity is unique among world belief systems. It gives us every reason to not fear death, while at the same time providing us equal reason to cherish life. When we see both, we can see the incredible love of a God whose love is perfect.

* * * * *

Kimberly was the first person to ask the question. Many others, after learning that I had been through a near-death experience, would ask as well. They wanted to know whether I had experienced the bright light or some other manifestation of an after-life reality. No matter how the question was worded, the actual query was obvious to me: "Did you have an experience that proves there is life after death?" I think, in essence, what each person wanted to know was whether what had happened to me "proved" that God exists. I had to disappoint them all, until about three months after my heart attack.

I awakened myself with my own screams: "No, please, please, let me go!" I did not immediately identify my experience as a dream; it was much too vivid, too real. My heart raced as I sat in my bed, unnerved. I tried to thrust myself back into the experience of the dream rather than accept the reality that had called me from it. I almost never dream, or at least never remember my dreams. This one was more profoundly "real" than any I had ever experienced.

In my dream, I relived the night I had collapsed on the ball field. I relived it, however, as a spectator, above the scene. I saw everything that had been described to me. I saw myself joking with Gino about his team not being able to hit my pitches. I watched as I collapsed on the mound, as Daryl rushed from third base and began CPR. I observed as Frank dashed from the clubhouse and Gino from his dugout to join the effort. I saw the other games stop and players from all those teams join my teammates in the outfield to pray. From my vantage point above the field, I saw Press on the phone with his wife as she called Nancy to tell her what had happened.

Long frantic minutes below me passed as casual seconds from my vantage point. The ambulance arrived, and the paramedics began to treat me. I saw my body spasm when they attached the pads and cardioverted. I observed their relief when the electricity worked and my heart returned to a perfusing rhythm.

I watched the frantic activity, as if a child who has kicked an ant hill, observing the rapid response of the insects to the invasion. Everywhere below me, words and actions reflected the fear and concern of my friends and of all those people of God who care for others. Only one soul was at peace—mine. Even as I watched my own body lying in the dirt, my soul was completely at rest, bathed in a soft warmth and yellowish light. Until the words filled my thoughts: "It's time to go back."

The words came with absolute quiet, but my response was an anguished shout: "Please, no!" I did not want to go back. I had never felt so much at peace, so rested. All I wanted was to continue, to leave that scene and everything of this world behind. And yet, I knew, my pleas would go unheeded.

I awakened shouting. I could not relax for long minutes as I replayed the dream. I wanted to curse God for giving me the glimpse He had shared. I loved Him for sending me back. My girls needed me. It was not my time. But I wanted it to be. No matter how much I might love my life and cherish all the moments that lay ahead to love my girls, in the darkness of my room, I wanted that feeling of peace and rest much more.

In the days and years that have followed, I have thought often about this "dream." It did not come to me like the after-life experiences often described. My experience came later. I did not see anything in my dream that had not been described to me already. No images formed that I had not already created during my visits with my teammates and friends. I cannot see my dream as having been a revelation to me, exactly. I am certain that the "reason" for my being sent back was that my daughters were not, as Kate had told Dr. Ahmed, going to lose both parents within a single year. What I wanted and what I was supposed to do may have been in conflict, but God has His plan, and our role is to embrace it.

Maybe it was just a dream, nothing more. If I did get a glimpse into the life that awaits us, then I do know for certain that it is a life of extraordinary comfort and joy. Joy so great that it could make me want to give up everything I cherish in my life and go with God.

The more important lesson for me that night, however, was

not that the lives we live now are insignificant. Rather, as I finally relaxed and thought about the vision, I realized that we are on earth for a reason; we live the lives we live as part of a greater plan. I learned also, however, that there is, and should be, joy in our lives. Yes, we do live to serve a greater plan. We live also, however, so that we can enjoy our lives, so that we can feel passion, so that our lives are vital.

I have never referred to my dream as having given me a memory of an after-life experience. It was a dream, both disturbing and comforting at the same time. It was not an after-life experience. It was not a message about what comes after we die. It was just the opposite. It was a message about how we should live. It told me to love this life!

Chapter Nine

Nighttime has a pronounced, sometimes profound, effect on many people. Situations that they find troubling during the daytime can become frightening at night. The pain that seemed little more than a touch of heartburn during the day quickly becomes a heart attack once the sun has gone down. Behavior that people avoid during the light of day somehow becomes more acceptable during the dark of night. The night can encourage people to act in ways that are dangerous. Darkness hides violent actions and gives cover to irresponsibility. It can encourage the insecure that their fears are valid. A nighttime dispatch tends to challenge EMS workers in one of two ways; it either challenges their medical skills or their patience. In either case, a call that comes in the middle of the night does much more than interrupt an emergency responder's sleep. Such a call requires rapidly becoming alert and caring.

Bo and I received such a call at approximately 2:00 a.m. in the middle of a rain storm. Dispatch indicated we were responding to a female down, with a possible compound fracture, one which would present with the broken bone penetrating the skin. Rarely does such a dispatch prove to be accurate. Such a grim outlook is more often the result of the over reaction of a shaken caller than it is an accurate assessment of the patient's condition. Dispatch did not send a fire unit in support, and I chose not to wake up three more responders in the middle of the night, certainly not a rainy night.

I should have remembered the advice of my supervisor: "Jerry, you're in the asking business. Dispatch is in the getting business." As soon as I saw our patient, a tall stout lady, probably approaching three hundred pounds, lying in the mud, illuminated by flood lights from her house, with our only access to her with the cot being along a steep and rain-soaked grassy bank, I knew my mistake. Her left ankle did not have an open wound with a bone protruding, but it was snapped sideways at a ninety degree angle, with the broken end of the bone snug against the skin and ready to break through at any moment. She had slipped on a wet sidewalk along the back of her house so that her full weight had shifted onto the fractured ankle. Her pain was intense. She wailed behind the curtain of her soaked blonde hair.

Bo returned to the truck to call for a fire unit to assist and to navigate our cot back to our patient. I hurried ahead to get a long board. Our patient's children, two beautiful little blonde toddlers, stood at the back door watching their mother struggle with her pain, their blue eyes as wide as an owl's. Her husband stood looking helpless until I grabbed him to help me. The only positive thing I found during a rapid assessment of the injury was that she had a pulse, therefore circulation, distal to the injury. Her toes were receiving blood, and whatever else we did moving her we had to be sure that we did not compromise that circulation, which meant if at all possible not letting that broken bone break the skin or move so that she lost circulation to her foot.

Our patient continued to wail as we first moved her gently along the ground away from a series of steps so that we could lay her flat on her back. Though each movement must have increased her pain, she maintained an amazingly cooperative attitude. She screamed, she cursed, she sounded like a banshee, but not once did she indicate she was not ready for us to do what we had to do. When Bo, her husband, and I finally had to slide her onto the long board, however, she let loose: "Oh damn you, damn you, that hurts. Oh, I am so sorry. I am so sorry. I don't talk like that. I am so sorry." Another movement. "Oh damn you, all of you. I am so sorry. I don't talk like that. I am so sorry."

"Lady, you shout all you want," I said. "Just please know I am trying not to hurt you."

"I know," she whispered through clinched teeth and rapid breathing.

Once we had her secured to the long board, Bo and I lifted her to the cot and secured her further. The long board provided as much of a splint as I wanted to use for the moment. Once we had her loaded, I could give morphine and then try to snug the ankle in a pillow splint after her pain had eased.

We still had no fire unit on scene, but had found a capable helper in her husband, so I decided to try and edge her along the bank and to our truck. When Bo and I lifted the cot, however, it did not lock in raised position and her weight pulled us back to its lowered position. My back screamed. So did our patient. "Oh damn you, damn you, that hurts. Oh, I am so sorry. I am so sorry. I don't talk like that. I am so sorry."

"It's OK," I said as Bo and I tried again, this time successfully to raise the cot.

Slowly the three of us negotiated the bank and managed to get the cot to our truck, just as the fire unit, with my supervisor Jay on board, arrived. As Bo and I went to work placing our patient on oxygen and the cardiac monitor, getting vitals, and working to gain IV access, I noticed three sleepy faces staring in the back of the truck. Their eyes were half closed and their clothes quickly matting to their skin from the pouring rain. All three expressions asked, "Why did you call us out in the rain?"

I could hear their *unspoken* screams: "Oh damn you, damn you, we were asleep. We're not sorry. We do talk like that!"

"Thanks, guys," I said. "I think we've got it."

Of course, they were put of bed at this point and jumped in to help us splint our patient's foot, leading to another stream of "Oh damn you, damn you, that hurts. Oh, I am so sorry. I am so sorry. I don't talk like that. I am so sorry."

Jay, with his usual tact, responded, "That's alright. You scream. It hurts me just looking at it."

"Oh damn you!" she responded. This time without apology.

As quickly as we were in route, I gave my patient morphine for pain and promethazine for nausea. The morphine did not, however, have as much effect as I would have hoped. Despite that fact, my patient maintained an amazingly gracious response. She screamed when the truck bounced. Cursed a few times. Apologized with each curse. She responded with an amazingly good will, despite having sustained such a serious and painful injury. She was well aware from looking at her foot that she was facing surgery and a lengthy rehabilitation period.

As an EMS responder I have carried many patients who called 911 for a minor pain, hoping that the ER doctor will give them drugs. I have transported far more patients who would have been as well served by a cab ride as an ambulance transport. Many of those patients have acted as if somehow their minor health concern is a major and life-threatening emergency. As a result of my interaction with such patients I have developed a profound respect for those, such as my patient with the ankle fracture, who have conducted themselves with such grace. As quickly as her curses served as a reminder that God's children have their frailties, her apologies testified to the fact that we are, in the end, "created in His image." For such a patient, a ninth Beatitude might be appropriate: Blessed are those who curse in their pain, for in their apology for their cursing is their spirit truly revealed.

*****

Getting out of the rehab hospital proved to be much more difficult than getting in. By the time Heather had all the paperwork finished and the out-patient arrangements made for my discharge on Thursday and Kimberly had driven me home, the day was almost gone. I settled in on the sofa, as she left for her night shift at the steak house. Kate was still completing her afternoon shift. I had insisted that they both not take time away from work because of my situation. After Kimberly left, I settled back into the softness of the sofa and looked around my house, examining photographs that had probably received no more than a passing glance for years and finding a sense of wonder at the blessings which they recorded from my life, my children and the many adventures we had shared.

The quiet lasted only a few minutes as Steve stopped by to check on me. He had gone to the hospital, learned that I had been discharged, and came directly to the house. Within an hour, Steve had passed along all the news about our friends and co-workers, about his family, about his recent vacation. Then Steve told me the story of my collapse and recovery from his vantage point, the way a friend would, without holding back to protect my feelings. I finally learned what had happened without the overlay of gentleness that others had used to gloss the difficult-to-hear details. To some, that might seem an almost cruel level of detail. For me it was necessary--necessary to learn how beaten I had looked when on the ventilator, how swollen when my kidneys had shut down and my body began retaining fluid. He told me about the fear and the courage he had seen in the girls, about their fear and their desperation, about how defeated they had seemed at times. Steve relayed to me just how often he had been contacted by the people we worked with, and those with whom we had played ball during past seasons as friends and people I hardly knew, alike, had asked for updates on my condition. From others, I had learned my story in broad strokes.

Steve provided the color and the fine lines so that the picture became more vivid, more real. Steve knew me well enough, our friendship was close enough, that he was not going to let me go any longer with unanswered questions. He trusted me to have the emotional strength to deal with the facts—to cope with the truth.

As Steve talked, my mind drifted back, back over the past few weeks, and then back almost thirty years. My journey into the past was interrupted, however, as Kate burst through the door, and I sensed that finally things were back where they needed to be. Steve slipped out as Kate and I had our chance to celebrate our family's victory. I was overwhelmed by my feelings, by being able to hug her and tell her that our life was going to return to normal. I told her that she did not have to worry about her father any longer. We hugged. We cried. We celebrated. I was proud that she and Kimberly had continued as much as possible with their lives while I was in the hospital, even that Kate had worked her shift the day I was released. I was also pleased, however, that she stayed at home that night until, as always, she retired to her room upstairs around 9:00 p.m., to visit with her friends on the computer and continue with her life's routine. In the quiet, however, I continued with my earlier reflections about another emotionally charged day, followed by a quiet evening of reflection.

* * * * *

In 1974, I was twenty years old and working for the summer on a demolition crew. My team had been gutting an old wing of Baptist Hospital in Winston-Salem. To gut it meant taking out everything within the concrete shell. We spent most of our time using sledge hammers, shovels, and wheel barrows, breaking, loading, and hauling thousands of tons of rubble. By the time our Friday afternoons arrived, all of us were worn out from the week.

The third week in July had been especially demanding for me. The week before my father had suffered a heart attack. Although he had progressed well, the added stress had fueled my impatience with everything I was doing, both at home and at work. That impatience demanded a price. When I attempted to undercut and then bring down too large a section of wall, it dropped before I was ready and buried me under a pile of concrete block and ceramic tile. I was unconscious only briefly. When I awoke, I heard my co-workers clearing the rubble. The pieces of wall were too large to lift. Each hammer blow they delivered shook the pieces that lay across my back and legs.

"Jerry?" I heard the voice of my boss, Brian Miller, calling.

"Yeah."

"We'll have you out in another minute or two."

"I can't see, Brian," I said, my mouth so full of dust I could barely croak my words.

"Just hold on, we have doctors from the hospital already here."

The fact that we were working on an old wing of a hospital proved good luck. Doctors and nurses had been pulled from the adjoining wing to be ready to care for me. I was unable to see anything, but did hear a strong masculine voice tell Brian that I would probably have a broken back.

"I can feel my legs!" I shouted.

"We're almost to you," Brian said. "Just don't try to move."

"I can't move, but I can feel my legs!"

As the last of the wall was lifted, hands reached under my twisted frame and carried me to a gurney.

"I can't see," I said again.

"You just have a lot of blood in your eyes," Brian told me. "It's not a problem."

A doctor began to conduct a trauma assessment, that authoritative voice I had heard earlier talking to someone as he went: "Possible spinal damage and internal organ injuries. Left arm appears fractured at the elbow. Significant lacerations to the scalp..." He rattled it off in a monotone as the gurney was hurried through the hallways to the emergency room.

After four hours of x-rays and stitches—over a hundred to my face and scalp—I walked from the emergency room. My mother had been visiting my father when the accident occurred. Brian had found her, told her about the accident, and stayed with her while I was in the ER.

We rode to the house in quiet. I was aching and weary, but lines etched in my mother's face and the constant twitching of her fingers reflected more than exhaustion; they showed fear. At the house, I went to my room. I had seen my face in a mirror at the ER and didn't want a second look. Even more, however, I did not want to spend the evening seeing in my mother's face what the last week had done to her.

The quiet of my room was much like the stillness in my home the night after Kimberly brought me home from the rehabilitation hospital. It was a demanding quiet, a quiet that left me assessing my life, just as I had in 1974. At age nineteen, I had been only modestly able to appreciate how close I had come to being killed, although my youthful sense of invulnerability would be forever gone.

I turned on the radio after shutting the door to my room. When Kris Kristopherson's current hit, "Why me, Lord?" began to play, I cried for the first time that day. The significance of the question in those lyrics was so completely manifest in my experience that day that I could not hold back the tears which spoke my answer: "I don't know why me." Almost thirty years later, at a very different point in my life, that very same question came to me on an equally quiet night after a similarly remarkable event. And my answer had not changed: "I don't know why me. I especially don't know why me twice in one lifetime."

Ultimately, for all of us, when we find ourselves asking "why" about God's plan, we must be prepared to accept that answer, "I don't know," and to be comfortable with the fact that we don't know. But not knowing, while acting as confidently as if we possessed knowledge, is the essence of being a Christian. Accepting by faith is all God asks of us. He asks us to accept by faith when we have been spared, as I have been twice in my life. He asks us to accept by faith when we have suffered and are suffering. That kind of complete commitment to faith should come easy to someone like me who has dodged death, not once, but twice--who has overcome odds that would intimidate a Las Vegas gambler.

For the Musick family, however, whose faith has stood firm while watching Sami fight to recover from massive injuries--that faith demands celebration. Based on the science of her condition, their daughter will never fully recover. Based on the science of her injury, she should never have survived the accident. The Musick family, however, possesses the kind of faith that looks past what science says cannot happen, to hear the voice of God telling them what, because of their faith, can happen. What is amazing and uplifting is that throughout their struggle, the one constant has been their love for God and their faith in His goodness.

I have twice cried in the quiet of the night to think that God has spared me. Those tears have held joy on both occasions. I am sure that the Musick family has shed many tears as well. What amazes me about them, however, about all who love God during their trials, is how completely firm their faith has stood, has allowed them to dry their tears, and has enabled them to find joy in what God has given them, not despair over what they have lost. Their faith is the truest celebration of a loving God I have ever witnessed. Their faith speaks many messages, none more true than the message that God wants us to live our lives fully, not in fear for what it may bring, but with joy for what it does bring—the opportunity to love God and live an essential life.

* * * * *

Six months after I was released from the hospital, spring arrived, the grass turned green, and softball practice for the Aldersgate team began. During that six months I had continued an extensive exercise regiment. It began in July with my walking up and down my driveway several times each day. By Christmas, I was walking several miles, twice a day, wearing ankle weights to intensify the cardiovascular effort required by my walking. I had, however, also suffered setbacks, including two additional stint procedures to deal with the scar tissue that kept developing on the stints Dr. Wool had placed in my damaged artery in the days following my heart attack. By February, however, I was ready for spring practice.

Kate was not. She was equally certain about my plans; she was emphatic that I had no business playing softball. We compromised. I would coach the team. As soon as I went to the first practice, put on my cleats, and listened to the music of their clatter as I walked across the parking lot to the field, felt the embrace of my well-oiled glove, smelled the new grass of spring and the damp earth of the infield, I knew that I would be playing. I had to play. Playing softball again would be the final step to healing, not my body, but my spirit. For the past several months I had lived with fear. For me to live a complete life, I would have to place the fear behind me and God's promise of a full life before me.

During that first practice, I had to reassure my teammates who had watched me collapse on the mound nine months earlier that I was ready to play. Some of them were as reluctant as my daughter. As a result of my walking and other cardiovascular work during the summer and fall, however, if anything I was in better playing condition than I had been the previous spring. I had quit smoking and maintained a healthier diet. My weight was down and my endurance improved. I felt good as I pitched batting practice and then hit fielding practice. I managed to dispel some of the doubts my teammates felt.

The two hours of practice that afternoon made me feel alive, joyful to be living in the moment. I went home exhausted and exhilarated, eager for the next practice and anticipating the first game like a child waiting for Christmas morning. That evening, as I prepared our supper, Kate sat at the breakfast bar observing me. I felt her gaze and knew she was looking for any signs that I had over exerted.

"I'm going to coach the team. OK?"

She did not seem impressed. Her doubts were well-founded.

Six weeks later, opening night arrived, and our first game was back at the park where I had collapsed. As I prepared to leave and she saw me in the team shirt, Kate again let me know her feelings.

"I knew you were going to play."

The matter seemed simple. Was I going to play in a church-league softball game? Kate saw nothing simple in it. I looked into her green eyes and saw fear, the kind of fear that develops in a child who has watched her mother die and her father lie within death's grasp. She was sixteen and knew that really bad things do happen to children. She understood what it felt like to see everything secure in her life collapse. My playing softball again was as symbolic for her as it was for me. In that moment, what meant life for me represented death to her. I had to choose the joy of living over the fear of dying. I had to act with confidence in the promise of God, as spoken in Isaiah, "fear not, for I am with you, be not dismayed, for I am your God; I will strengthen you, I will help you, I will uphold you with my victorious right hand" (41:10).

If playing softball on that April night represented a completion for me, the final step in my recovery, the fact that we were playing the same team we had been playing the night of my heart attack only underscored this fact. Ours was the first game of the night, so we warmed up on the field itself rather than at one of the practice areas. We completed warm-ups and both teams lined up along the base lines for prayer. I watched for Geno, but for whatever reason he was not with his team that night.

As the prayer ended, a tall black man from the other team jogged across the field.

"You're the guy . . ."

"I'm the guy," I answered.

"I told those guys; I told them while your team was warming up."

He smiled broadly, as the well-built athlete lit up like a child. I teared up for the first time that evening. And there in the fresh spring air as night began to descend, just a few yards from the pitcher's mound, two of God's children embraced and celebrated His goodness with no further words. None were needed. And perhaps it is worth a footnote to this narrative to point out that this embrace between a black man and a white man, both children of God, occurred in Montgomery, Alabama, where, regardless of its history, people of faith, of all races, do, as God asks, love each other.

I played two innings that night, dove for one ground ball so that I went home with dirt on my shirt. Under raised eyebrows Kate stared at me with expressionless eyes. I remember those eyes but then consider how for nine years she lived a life of chasing dreams, facing her setbacks, and celebrating her victories. She has lived a vital life, a life not without fear, but with fear always in check. And in the way she has lived as much as the way I have lived, I know that God intended for me to return to the softball field, just as He intended for me to return to my life, to live it fully, to become a paramedic, to meet JeDonne and enjoy a marriage full of love, to not let the fear of dying ever prevent me from knowing the joy of living.

Chapter Ten

If you are now reading this chapter, then I was able to finish a book that has been a struggle to write, that has forced me to revisit some of the most difficult moments in my life and to soberly reflect on mistakes I have made and shortcomings in my character that have led to those mistakes. I am, as I write, approximately half way through composing the story I wish to tell. February 8, 2010 gave me the experience, which better than any I have yet had in my life, illustrates what lies at the end of my journey, both as a person who loves God and as a writer, so I am bypassing the linear path of composition in order to write about that experience while it lies fresh in my mind and deep in my soul.

At approximately 18:00, February 8, 2010, Dispatch called the Crew with a location and the words "major MVC." I had never heard Dispatch characterize a car wreck. My partner, Bo, and I rolled the ambulance, while two other Crew members, Mark and Josh, brought our heavy rescue truck. Three or four minutes later, I crawled into a crumpled sedan that had been involved in a high-speed--as it would turn out over one hundred miles per hour—front-end collision. I found a thirty-six-year-old woman pinned in the driver's seat. Her body was pushed to the left, and her head lay limp on her left shoulder. She had no pulse. Her pupils were dilated and fixed. Frigid air blew in through the shattered window. The crew from our heavy rescue truck and firefighters had arrived on scene, moved into position, and were ready to unload the "jaws." I knew the men on the fire truck; they would have had her out in just minutes. I looked at them, caught their expectant eyes, and shook my head. I crawled out, asked that they cover her with a sheet from the ambulance, moved to the next patient, and left the mother of two teenage daughters without further treatment. She had, in all likelihood, died on impact. She could not be resuscitated.

This book began with a little girl, who survived a MVC and began a journey to recovery that has been filled with miracles. It ends with a mother of two daughters whose life was lost in a MVC caused by a nineteen-year-old who was drag racing on a city street and whom I treated for minor injuries before turning him over to a Fire Department ambulance crew from a mutual support agency who transported him to the hospital. Bo and I then treated the passenger in his car and transported him as well. Police began a rigorous search for the other car involved in the incident but whose driver had fled the scene.

The events of that February evening provide no evidence that we can find justice in this world, not the kind of justice that we can understand. Nothing that happens in the courts addressing the cause of the wreck can do anything other than illustrate the gap between what we can do in the name of justice and what we think justice demands. Much more important, however, those events challenge us to believe that God is with us at every moment in our lives, during the times of our greatest joy as well as those of our most profound sorrow. With firefighters ready to remove my patient from that car, with the skills to do it rapidly, all I needed was just the slightest of signs that my patient could be worked, and I would have made a different decision. I knew exactly what protocol to follow, trusted my skills to perform every action within those protocols, and had the help on scene to treat her rapidly and effectively. I have to dip deeply into my efforts to keep faith to not challenge God by asking whether He was in fact there with me, with my patient, for not giving all of us on that scene at least the slimmest of hopes. That, however, was not God's plan, and, instead, He left me with the challenge of accepting that He, not I, has the power over life and death. My obligation as a person of faith is to accept His will, not to change it.

Later that night, when I learned that my patient had two teenage daughters, I realized that this call would become the basis of my final words in this book. I know from watching my two daughters lose their mother when they were young what lies ahead for those two girls. Teenage girls need their mothers. They need what a woman has to offer. Nothing, no person, not a father, not a stepmother, not a grandmother, will be able to give them the comfort they need during the difficult moments or the celebratory hugs they seek during the good ones the way their mother would have been able to. As teenagers, even more than would a younger or an older daughter, they will experience the loss of their mother. Knowing what they face from watching my girls deal with their anger and their sadness in the days, weeks, months, and even years after made me want to rage at God for not being on that scene. He had been with Sami. He had been with me in 2001. He had been with many of my patients in ways that were obvious and thus allowed me to "know" He was on the scene with all my patients when it was less obvious. From those experiences I had grown to accept that He had even been with my daughters when they lost their mother and nearly lost me. The irony becomes obvious that I could be writing a book about faith and prayer and during the very writing of that book find my faith pushed to the edge when I found myself thinking about my daughters and their loss. Thinking about them, however, brought me back from that edge.

Despite everything they suffered, in spite of all my anger that they had to endure and accept their loss, my daughters, more than anything or anyone else, have proven to me that our faith in God's presence is warranted, no matter what happens.

My Kimberly did not have her mother with her the day she married Shane, nor has she had her mother's love, offering words of encouragement as she has raised her own two daughters. She has, however, built a strong marriage and proved herself a loving and able mother. She did not have her mother to watch her receive her college diploma when she returned to school and balanced work, family, and classes. She did not have her mother to encourage her return to the church, but she did return to the family of God and is raising her children as Christians. I cannot say that she turned her loss into a gain, but she has, with strength of character, refused to let that loss prevent her from living a life that has made her father proud, as it no doubt makes her mother proud from her superior vantage point.

Kate was younger when her mother died. It was many years later when I finally saw her break into tears and say "it isn't fair" that she lost the experiences of having a mother. During all that time that she was carrying her grief, however, she was living a magnificent life. She won awards in high school and college for her singing. She graduated with honors from one of the finest prep schools in Alabama, received numerous scholarship offers from outstanding colleges and universities, and graduated from college *magna cum laude*. She has managed to do something amazing by following her dream to be an actor, living and working in Atlanta to keep her dream alive, and paying her bills while doing so! She lives a full life, filled with friends and ambition. She has even been able to open her heart and find in my second wife, JeDonne, a kind of love that allows her to send mother's day cards, noting that she is unable to find a "wicked stepmother" mother's day card.

As I write, two young girls are beginning their new lives, lives without their mother. They will never lose the pain or regain what they have lost. They will likely not find a substitute for their mother, and they will struggle with the senseless way their mother died. By seeing how my daughters have lived their lives, however, I have been able to see that God has been and remains with them. I am, therefore, able to find my faith that God will be with us all, including two teenage girls who will desperately need Him.

Ultimately, no matter how much I struggled to see God on February 8, 2010, I walked away from those events with the faith that when responding to EMS calls, I am, and will remain, never alone in the back.

Epilogue

In June 2010, 15 months after the accident that so seriously injured her, Sami and Coach Dunham of her school squared off in a tricycle race to raise money for victims of head injuries. That Sami had even enrolled in school the previous fall testifies to the miracle of her life. That she had during the previous months of therapy developed the physical skills to ride a tricycle and the cognitive and emotional capacity to do so fully engaged in the competition only underscores the rewards which she and her family have earned for their faith. Using the Internet site CaringBridge.com, Sami's family has shared their journey with all of us whose lives have been touched by their courage. Two entries written by Sami's mother on June 24, 2010 provide much better closing for this narrative than I could imagine offering myself and so I gratefully turn the final words over to her:

> On June the 7th Sami had her big race against Coach Dunham. It was great she enjoyed every minute of it. Some people viewed it as no big deal but we view it as a very big deal because of the reports we (had) gotten when we had the accident said she would not live and if she did she would be a vegetable. She is not a vegetable(;) she is very active, still needs help but is making leaps and bounds.

And finally, also from June 24, 2010:

> I want every one to know life is full of obstacles(;) what we do and how we react is how we can overcome these obstacles! So everyone have faith

and live a happy, joyful life. Live like there's no tomorrow. God wants us happy and worry free. Everyone be blessed. We are so very much blessed!! People think I'm a little crazy when I say these things but I am blessed. My child is alive and well. A happy little girl, that is full of life even when she has obstacles in her way. God is so great, everyone be blessed, I am!!!!

We do indeed serve a great and loving God! A God who has never, never left me alone in the back of an ambulance!

CPSIA information can be obtained at www.ICGtesting.com
260165BV00001B/2/P